Post-Secondary Education on the Edge

Norm Denzin
General Editor

Vol. 3

PETER LANG
New York • Washington, D.C./Baltimore • Bern
Frankfurt am Main • Berlin • Brussels • Vienna • Oxford

Jane McEldowney Jensen

Post-Secondary Education on the Edge

Self-Improvement and Community Development in a Cape Breton Coal Town

PETER LANG
New York • Washington, D.C./Baltimore • Bern
Frankfurt am Main • Berlin • Brussels • Vienna • Oxford

Library of Congress Cataloging-in-Publication Data

Jensen, Jane McEldowney.
Post-secondary education on the edge: self-improvement and community development in a Cape Breton coal town / Jane McEldowney Jensen.
p. cm. — (Cultural critique; v. 3)
Includes bibliographical references and index.
1. Postsecondary education—Social aspects—Nova Scotia—Cape Breton Island—Case studies. 2. Self-culture—Nova Scotia—Cape Breton Island—Case studies. 3. Community development—Nova Scotia—Cape Breton Island—Case studies.
I. Title: Postsecondary education on the edge. II. Title. III. Series.
LC1039.8.C22 C365   378.716'95—dc21   2002022496
ISBN 0-8204-5546-6
ISSN 1530-9568

Die Deutsche Bibliothek-CIP-Einheitsaufnahme

Jensen, Jane McEldowney:
Post-secondary education on the edge: self-improvement and community development in a Cape Breton coal town / Jane McEldowney Jensen.
–New York; Washington, D.C./Baltimore; Bern;
Frankfurt am Main; Berlin; Brussels; Vienna; Oxford: Lang.
(Cultural critique; Vol. 3)
ISBN 0-8204-5546-6

Cover art reproduces a painting of Glace Bay by Kenny Boone, *Untitled*, (1994)
Cover design by Lisa Barfield

© 2002 Peter Lang Publishing, Inc., New York

All rights reserved.
Reprint or reproduction, even partially, in all forms such as microfilm, xerography, microfiche, microcard, and offset strictly prohibited.

In Cape Breton
By LeRoy Payne Peach

No trains, no local T.V.,
No Air Canada jets,
No free trade, no fish—
Abandonment, exploitation.

But what the heck
We still have the sea,
The harmonious headlands,
The seven-fold amen
Of the land itself,
Saturday night at the local pub,
Tag days at the liquor store,
The grant (much reduced mind you),
Ceilidhs everywhere.

Above all our sense of humour.

The politicians will never
Figure out how to take that
Away from us.

ACKNOWLEDGMENTS

I wish to thank all the people who contributed to this work. First and foremost I want to express my gratitude to the people of Cape Breton who made this research possible. Acquaintances, friends, and students all offered me, knowingly or not, their insights on life in Glace Bay and made me feel welcome. I am also grateful to the Fulbright Foundation and the Canadian Embassy for their financial support.

I also wish to thank Carol Greenhouse for helping me through this project and making the extra effort to cross disciplinary lines. This research was, from the beginning, a rite of passage as I traveled from one academic field to another and then back again through my fieldwork. I am also obliged to all those who listened and commented upon earlier workings of this project, especially Joyce Canaan, Wesley Shumar, and Bryan Brayboy.

Most of all I would like to thank my husband, Mark, my daughter, Ella, and my extended family. I often envied my Cape Breton friends' confidence in the power of kin, near and extended, to sustain. Now that I have my own family, I have come to realize how wise they were.

Grateful acknowledgment is made to LeRoy Payne Peach for permission to include "In Cape Breton," reprinted from *Inlets of the Heart*, published by UCCB Press. I also appreciate the talents of Kenny Boone and his generosity in the use of his artwork, *View of Glace Bay*, on the cover.

 # TABLE OF CONTENTS

Chapter 1: "Come from Away" 1
    Superstition of Rarity 6
    Aspirations and Educational Consciousness 9
    Cape Breton: A Rock in the Stream 12
    Living in Cape Breton 14
    Organization of the Text 16

Chapter 2: "From the Bay" 19
    Black Around the Eyes: A History of Coal 23
    Glace Bay Identity 28
    The Politics of Class: "Us" and "Them" 36

Chapter 3: "No Burden to Carry" 43
    Popular Education 45
    Going to University: Higher Education in Glace Bay 53
    "Our Young Fella": Educational Aspirations 58
    The High School on the Highway 64
    Conclusion: Shifting the Burden 67

Chapter 4: "Training for What?" 71
    Human Capital Development 72
    Education as Big Business 78
    The "Pogie": Education as Unemployment Insurance 79
    The TAGS Program: A Case Study 85
    Conclusion 92

Chapter 5: Local Literacy 97
    Everyday Literacy 100
    Applying Local Wisdom: Decision-Making 109
    Multiple Literacies: Insiders and Outsiders 113
    Authority and Expertise: The Limits of Local Literacy 118
    Conclusion 123

Chapter 6: Barbarians at the Gate 125
    Community *Ceilidh* 128
    Living "Away" 131
    Imported Knowledge 133
    Local Learning 134
    Death of the King 137

Bibliography 139

Index 147

CHAPTER 1
"Come from Away"

Ciad Mille Failté
(One Hundred Thousand Welcomes)

The first time I drove to Cape Breton Island, I stopped at a gas station on the mainland about an hour outside of Halifax, Nova Scotia. The attendant asked if I was on vacation. I grew up in Vermont where tourists are a necessary but sometimes irritating commodity, and I hated the idea of being lumped among them. "I'm an anthropologist," I told the attendant, desperately trying to get rid of my tourist identity, "going to Cape Breton to study education." He began to laugh. With a Gaelic brogue and plaid tam o'shanter, the man was a living caricature of a Scottish highlander, the kind of figure that gets printed on hand towels to be sold to people from Toronto and Boston, but his opinion of Cape Bretoners was filled with modern cynicism. "Good luck with them," he said, "they need all the education they can get!" With that he took my money and walked back into his station, muttering in Gaelic.

I was on my way to the town of Glace Bay, located in the southeastern corner of Cape Breton, a coal-mining town not usually chosen as a vacation destination except by expatriates returning home to visit family. Not many people think of industry when they think of Cape Breton. Media promotions, travel brochures, and calendar art depict the island as the highland heart of Canada, and the island's national park is well known for its natural beauty. Rarely is the industrial landscape of the southeastern coast part of the picture. In another encounter with mainland attitudes, I was chatting with a waitress in a restaurant along the popular southern shore of Nova Scotia. "They have the highest rate of family violence in Canada," she exclaimed when I told her I was going to live in Glace Bay and seemed astonished that I would want to go there at all. Her information was incorrect, but despite this, it was clear that Cape Breton's reputation as less than civilized was well established. News stories covering poverty and unemployment in the Maritimes highlight the negative side of Atlantic Canada's economy. The artifacts of that poverty: violence, alcoholism, and depression are indeed part of Cape Breton's national reputation.

What initially attracted me to Cape Breton were descriptions provided by friends and family of the vibrant cultural life of the island despite deep economic distress. Glace Bay was and is familiar to anyone who has lived in or driven through an industrial neighborhood—rows of plain box houses with corner markets and the occasional video store. The lives of Glace Bay residents are also familiar. The people who live there go to work (or to the unemployment office), send their children to school, care for their older relatives and friends, and enjoy one another's company. In many ways, Glace Bay is no different from thousands of other working-class communities, and yet its location on the edge of a continent, on an island known for natural beauty and persistent poverty, makes it unique. But is it?

Saskia Sassen (1991) claims that, despite and because of massive changes in technology and global economics, industrial nations are caught in a duality between advanced and backward economic practices. Sassen describes new geographies of centers and margins created by the service economy. Within the core of what she calls the new economic centers—the cities—there are abandoned or marginalized spaces in which displaced workers endure. I would argue that there are abandoned or marginalized spaces throughout the postindustrial landscape of so-called advanced nations, places like colliery towns, factory neighborhoods, and industrial communities of all shapes and sizes. Some of these places are found on the edges of metropolitan areas, forming an industrial border between urban and rural, exhibiting characteristics of both. Others, like Glace Bay, are found in remote locations, mountains and deserts, connected by railroads and highways to centers of commerce but tied economically, politically, and socially to regional hubs. The modern era of industry has shaped most of North America, even those places we think of as traditional or separate (Eller, 1982). This postindustrial abandonment has resulted in the reordering of people as "evicted populations" move and local cultures transform (Harvey, 2000). In a postindustrial economy, the residents of such communities are forced to redefine themselves and their sense of place.

Glace Bay, Nova Scotia, is one of these abandoned spaces. A small fishing community that became "the biggest town in Canada" as a result of the coal-mining industry;[1] Glace Bay is located about four hours east of the city of Halifax in a region that has produced coal for global markets since the 1700s.[2] Glace Bay is similar to towns and neighborhoods across North America that were and are dependent upon single industries and the absentee ownership of production or extraction. This study joins other ethnographic community studies in examining how the residents of such working-class communities construct their place within the processes of capitalism. For example, Nash (1989) describes the effects of industrial change on community and family in Pittsfield, Massachusetts, in her work, *From Tanktown to High Tech*. Similarly, in *The Magic City*, Pappas (1989) explores the experiences of the unemployed in the rubber-manufacturing town of Barberton, Ohio. These studies share the task of not only describing a place but also imbedding the cultural practices of local residents in a larger economic and political context, particularly the end of modern industrial capitalism (Ortner, 1991). Places like Glace Bay, Barberton, and Pittsfield, which were once centers of industrial production, are now on the margins of a global service economy. To "come from away" in Glace Bay means that you are not local, regardless of how far you have come or who you are.

I came to Glace Bay to study education. I was particularly interested in examining how government strategies to alleviate the troubled economy through increased educational achievement were perceived by local residents. This book is about the social construction of education, specifically post-secondary education, but not any one particular institution or school. Instead, I try to imagine education as what Bourdieu would call a set of "propositions possessing potential applicability...as elements of values and knowledge in a culturally plural and institutionally diverse society" (Robbins, 1998, 48). A great deal of weight is put on the possibilities of education, but we often do not question our assumptions about that potential. Part of an anthropologist's job is to ask these kinds of questions. Making the familiar strange requires pointing out and critiquing the assumptions we have about the way the world we know works. It means turning an interpretive lens on that which we take for granted.

For example, writing about post-secondary education in North America for an educated readership means exposing a variety of assumptions. One assumption commonly held by those who have thus far succeeded in the educational system is that education is good. Why not? For those who are successful, education can open doors, provide opportunities, and enhance one's quality of life. It can provide what Gouldner (1979) describes as a culture of critical discourse that can be used by the holder to negotiate the power structure of society. But if education does all of these things and gives such power, then we might also assume that those who are not successful in school face closed doors, fewer opportunities, and a reduced quality of life. Is this true? Is it true in all contexts? Was it true in Glace Bay?

Education is often defined by rhetoric about achievement and success. For example, most people are familiar with the maxim "If you work hard you will get ahead." We encourage students to work hard so that they might achieve. Most of us are also familiar with the argument that increased educational achievement by the individual benefits society as a whole. According to an economic model of human capital, the higher the educational achievement levels in a region, the better the economic picture. Education holds the potential or promise of increased economic and social position relative to other individuals and/or other communities. Because of the rhetorical (not necessarily empirical) marriage between education and economic prosperity, we assume that education is needed, and in so doing we imply that formal education can provide something more, something different and better, than informal practices of local knowledge (Gabbard, 1998).

The assumption of need and the implication that something may be lacking in a particular place reinforce why we must study educational aspirations in context in order to understand how the potential of education is applied. This book, therefore, describes the ways that individuals living in a particular place define education and the production of knowledge. What kinds of knowledge or credentials do the residents of Glace Bay identify as necessary and for whom? If we assume that formal education offers something better than what is available through common sense or informal processes of learning, we infer that there is something inferior or at least inefficient about informal practices and local knowledge that education can alleviate. Glace Bay had and has high levels of educational achievement. Yet what good have those educational credentials done locally? What was considered useful knowledge in Glace Bay and why? For whom? Under what conditions? Without knowing what local knowledge sets contain or what kinds of knowledge are used within a particular locale, we cannot make assumptions about the efficacy of formal education.

We take for granted, therefore, that education is good. We aspire, as educated citizens, for more educational credentials, and we encourage those without to do the same. But what does this pursuit of education do for the family, the community, and the local setting that cannot, in effect, "own" the commodity of educational credentials earned by the individual? We can make the claim that an individual's credentials can be an asset to his or her community, but for industrial neighborhoods like Glace Bay such credentials were, perhaps, diamonds in too rough a context, assets with limited exchange value. Educational credentials thus became a sign that divided the community into haves and havenots—just as much as tangible commodities might but with less resale value.

What happens to communities undergoing economic transformations, where job markets are changing and requiring more formal training of one generation than of the last? What happens to the kinds of knowledge people use on an everyday basis outside of work? If education is regarded as necessary for success, then what good are existing kinds of knowledge production? By challenging our assumptions of the need for formal education in a particular community with its own intrinsic knowledge set, we find that education might not always be good (or at least not the way we thought). We find that the process of getting and spending might inadvertently be laying waste alternatives that are also valuable, such as informal practices of local knowledge that maintain community relationships. In effect, education might be as destructive a proposition to community survival as it is a positive proposition for the individual.

This book examines these questions of self-improvement and community development in a historically and economically specific context. Does the educational achievement of the individual always result in the improvement of the community? What does this development cost and for whom? I try to find the links between individual achievement and the sustainability of communities and the ways that education serves to create and destroy those links. These questions are at the heart of conversations we hear about economically vulnerable regions. How do we address the problems of "brain drain" or the out-migration of the young and educated? What is lost when individuals from rural or working-class communities assimilate into the suburban middle class? How do we solve the puzzle of survival for small towns that have little to offer big economies?

This study examines post-secondary educational aspirations in a town where gradual persistence by immigrant families produced remarkable academic achievement. There have been individuals with some post-secondary education in almost every Glace Bay family, and yet, for many residents who chose to stay in Cape Breton rather than leave to find work off the island, educational experiences have not protected them from the declining job market. Some found economic security in professional work that transcended the local economy, but then their children were often forced to leave. Some were forced into post-secondary training because of losing their job or government support, but with limited time and resources to pay for schooling, the benefits of that schooling were ambiguous.

The purpose of this book is not to argue that post-secondary education is useless or to criticize economic development efforts that attempt to capitalize on global trends. Neither do I wish to downplay or demean the importance of skills development or the benefits of general education. When I refer to education, I refer to educational programs, initiatives, and projects offered to adults after compulsory schooling. My objective is to question the assumptions that underlie our fascination with formal education as a panacea to our problems, to expose the hierarchical nature of post-secondary educational practices, and to highlight the very real benefits of local wisdom, everyday collaborative practices of learning and knowledge production, to sustainable development.

Superstition of Rarity

A hierarchical system of training certificates and educational credentials contains contradictions in that the efficacy of schooling is inherently tied to the unequal relations of capitalism. Individuals cling to their faith in progress. More than just a belief in the efficacy of schooling, education seems to hold a tantalizing sense of chance, what William Morris (in Morris, 1936) calls the "superstition of rarity," that promotes education as something that intrinsically improves the individual in ways that local or work experience cannot. All this despite compelling evidence that educational credentials will not always lead to success. In some ways, the underemployed and unemployed are still as vulnerable, despite their educational achievements, to the unequal relations of capitalism as were miners suffering under the coal operators of the early part of this century. Morris (in Morris, 1936), writing of education in turn of the century industrial England, argued that capitalism exploits education just as it does the production of labor:

> For just as the capitalists would at once capture this education in craftsmanship, search out what little advantage there is in it and then throw it away, so they do with all other education. A superstition still remains from the times when "education" was a rarity that it is a means for earning a superior livelihood; but as soon as it has ceased to be a rarity, competition takes care that education shall not raise wages; that general education shall be worth nothing, and that special education shall be worth just no more than a tolerable return on the money and time spent in acquiring it; and, mind you, such special education must be very carefully directed towards the one aim of commercial success in the specialty, or it will miss, and be thrown into the mass of general education which earns nothing. (p. 499)

For Glace Bay residents who strove to improve themselves, postsecondary educational credentials provided an edge that could not be found in a general high school education or on-the-job experiences, something that should have helped tip the balance in the search for opportunities. While making them more competitive in the job market, however, their credentials did not create exclusive opportunities for them. The credentialing system of education tends to reduce the cost-effectiveness of education as more people seek out and acquire credentials at each level (Collins, 1979).

Maude Barlow and Heather-jane Robertson (1994) call this commitment to the efficacy of schooling an ideological allegiance to transnational corporate values: competition, individualism, and technology. An allegiance to competitive technological models, according to Barlow and Robertson, is damning in that it is only the employers who benefit when there is an overeducated, unemployed population. Thus, there is an onslaught of pressure through pragmatic and ideological rhetoric to pursue what is not available through experience and local wisdom in order to gain credentials for a market that may or may not require them.

Morris's reference to the "superstition of rarity" reflects the shift from a preindustrial time of education for the very rich to a democratic ideology of educational opportunity but warns of the continued dominance of the forces of capitalism to reproduce social inequalities. Morris, writing before the beginning of the twentieth century, argues for the necessity of educating men to be men rather than workers. Barlow and Robertson's postindustrial analysis adds that our global society is drowning in information and starved for purpose, implying that education in a knowledge economy must focus on analytical skills, those of an educated rather than trained citizenry, to digest this information. What has changed? Although the conditions and nature of employment have changed, the paradox of education as a source of social transformation and a source of economic reproduction still exists.

These ideas were not new to Glace Bay: Early labor organizers demanded that miners be treated as men, fully capable of great success and accomplishment, rather than slaves. In the 1920s, labor leaders wanted to introduce a series of lectures given by "men of letters" that would raise the intellectual levels of individuals for the benefit of the community. They planned for the college library to hold resources where "men could read for themselves."[3] The "empowerment" of labor through education was made even more ambiguous by the conditions of de-industrialization, when training for work was not only "demeaning" but also ineffective due to the lack of work available. The value of education for self-improvement and the practice of training for work, while not exclusive for the individual, made vocational objectives for development initiatives problematic. Economic development was a very real need in Glace Bay, but without empowerment of local residents to improve their ability to plan their own strategies for personal and community improvement, the ambiguities of development programs continued to cloud more complex individual goals.

Local residents were aware of these difficulties. In a public meeting at the local university-college in the spring of 1993, intended to discuss how the institution could best serve the community, a retired miner stood and asked for a level of education that would provide for the enlightenment and betterment of the students rather than just training for work that did not exist. He said:

> When you came to us and said you were going to give us a university, we were excited. Finally, we would have our own place of learning that wasn't just an extension of some faraway university. But it didn't happen. You just gave us another training center where we would learn to do your work at your wage.

The bitterness of this comment reflects the paradox of education in marginalized regions facing ambiguous futures. Aspirations and expectations for success influence the decisions individuals make and their potential for "makin' it." But, fundamentally, we have not asked what it means to "make it."

Aspirations and Educational Consciousness

I try to understand educational decision-making as a process of awareness or consciousness of the social conditions that constrain an individual's choices. Consciousness is an important theoretical construct for understanding how decision-making or agency is neither a creation of an individual nor of society but a product of interdependent relations of power between the two. Consciousness is never static but develops from experience. Therefore, as Freire (1985) notes, "As men act upon the world effectively, transforming it by their work, their consciousness is in turn historically and culturally conditioned through the 'inversion of praxis'"(p. 71). Awareness or consciousness of the processes of knowledge acquisition and transmission (education) is historically contextualized. Educational consciousness develops through experiences and frames the strategies which individuals employ to improve themselves and their communities. Indeed, education as a form of knowledge production inscribes transformative effects or possibilities of change.

In addition, experiences occur within specific cultural contexts, what Bourdieu calls fields. We usually think of the field of education as defined by schools or at least instruction, but learning and self-improvement are part of the everyday fabric of living and therefore defy institutional ascription. In this way, the field of education is similar to the field of law, a set of norms, values, and practices that happen within and without institutional boundaries. Bourdieu describes law and education as social fields, as sites that require cultural capital for success but more broadly interpreted as sites of ideological contest in which "truths" are negotiated. When applied to the field of law, his theoretical insights provide a rich set of ideas with which to approach questions of definition and relations of power. Law and education hold a great deal in common as sites of cultural production.

For example, Merry (1991) describes the development of what she calls "legal consciousness" in her research with first-generation immigrants living in a working-class community in Massachusetts. Consciousness, in this case, refers to individuals' awareness of law as a set of values (i.e., their definition of what justice might mean) and as a structural context (i.e., the court, the magistrate's office, etc.). As people interact with the legal system, their legal consciousness develops—for better or worse—depending on their experiences. While their experiences may not be good ones, they have the potential for changing their "legal consciousness" as they engage in social interactions within institutional contexts:

> In general, people have the possibility of creativity and resistance, of changing their consciousness as they test it against the experiences of everyday life. (p. 5)

I would argue that people also develop an educational consciousness through their experiences with different contexts of learning. Law, according to Merry, "...has two edges: it is a source of domination and, at the same time, contains the possibilities of a challenge to that domination" (1991, p. 8). Critical research in education has demonstrated that the processes of education can also play a role of social domination, but if that is so, then, like law, education can also provide possibilities for contest (Apple, 1982; Carnoy, 1993; Willis, 1977).

Yngvesson (1993) also argues for the creative potential of individuals and the need to understand power as part of everyday processes rather than a separate inscribing construct imposed on individuals from above. Her research examines the resolution of conflict as an everyday practice in the processing of what the court calls "trouble cases" and the ways in which individuals consciously subvert the legal system. She reminds the reader that resistance produces relations of power as well as contests:

> The emphasis on subversion as contained by (and productive of) power is an important check on work that romanticizes resistance as evidence of a consciousness that is "outside" of power relations. But it is important as well not to collapse subversion into subjection, obscuring the potential for creativity and invention that is inherent in relations of power. (pp. 6-7)

Again, this view of individuals' interactions with the legal system demonstrates that individuals are neither victims nor winners but participants in an ongoing process of cultural production—not subjects but actors. Likewise, in discussing individuals' interactions with education, their strategies—whether successful in terms of reaching personal aspirations or not—can also be seen as acts which both produce and challenge power relations within society. Thus, education as a social field, as a site of ideological contest, includes the processes of schooling as well as everyday interactions in which knowledge is produced. Education, in this case, refers to the process of acquiring the skills and credentials necessary to meet aspirations for the future. This is not just a vocational process, but one in which multiple needs and hopes for the future are expressed. Aspirations give tangible evidence of educational consciousness. MacLeod (1995) states:

> Aspirations provide a conceptual link between structure and agency in that they are rooted firmly in individual proclivity (agency) but also are acutely sensitive to perceived societal constraints (structure). (p. 137)

What constraints (or opportunities) influenced changes in educational aspirations in Glace Bay? As residents achieved their aspirations, how did that success influence future generations? Conversely, if and when expectations for education waned, what effect did that have on the aspirations of others?

Glace Bay and the other colliery towns of Cape Breton are located on what travel magazines have called one of the most beautiful islands in the world. Getting out, moving up, and/or "makin' it" take on very different meanings for these kinds of communities. Although Glace Bay is a company town with industrial problems such as a lack of infrastructure and environmental issues, it shares enough of the good qualities of the surrounding rural landscape to give it value, aesthetically and socially, as a place to be from. The problems of community survival in the face of economic stress are easier to see in places like Glace Bay than in urban centers. When the mines close or the fisheries decline, we worry about the future of such places in ways we do not when a "slum" undergoes change. We do not talk about the need to maintain the cultural integrity of a housing project when we talk about improving the prospects of its children, but perhaps we should.

What do communities gain or lose when their residents succeed or fail? If educational institutions contribute to the reproduction of social stratification between groups, does educational achievement produce stratification within economically homogeneous communities? We know that children who grow up in low-income neighborhoods are less likely to do well in school than children from middle-income or suburban communities and that this affects their futures, but what kind of stratification happens within these settings? Can these differences also be explained by social characteristics, or are there other factors we have not considered? Finally, post-secondary education is rarely offered, with the exception of some community colleges, as local education. What effect, therefore, does the reproductive capacity of higher education have on local neighborhoods?

Perhaps one answer can be found in what we count as success. Although working-class communities tend to have lower educational achievement levels than their professional or middle-class counterparts, many children of working-class parents do succeed in school. Their success, however, is often inscribed in career choices that are, if not similar to those of their parents, then related to the life experiences of working-class families (i.e., nursing, teaching, accounting, etc.). Studies of the reproductive role of education in perpetuating social inequality help us understand why the processes of capitalism require this stratification of labor, but they do not address the evolution of educational aspirations within communities that are otherwise economically constrained.

Cape Breton: A Rock in the Stream

Nova Scotia is one of Canada's four Atlantic Provinces along with New Brunswick, Prince Edward Island, and Newfoundland. Central to this group, Nova Scotia is a gateway for summer visitors exploring the Maritimes, and tourism is a major part of the provincial economy. The island of Cape Breton is connected to the mainland by a causeway built in the late 1950s but has been a popular tourist destination since the 1930s due to its beautiful headlands overlooking the Atlantic. Rustic and raw, the Cape Breton highlands are indeed a taste of Scotland in the New World. Cape Breton's romantic image is largely a result of a 1930s anti-modernism tourism campaign which promoted an idealistic Victorian view of the Scottish highlander and the natural "untouched" beauty of the island (McKay, 1994). The promotion of a traditional "folk" heritage by the government resulted in continued support of traditional Gaelic culture.[4] Because of these protective policies, Cape Bretoners are well known internationally for maintaining traditional Gaelic practices of folklore and music. The islanders are very proud of this reputation.

The promotion of Cape Breton in the twenty-first century with romantic images of "traditional" highlanders in full tartan also appeals to the traditions and memories of the island's residents as romantic survivors of modern injustice.[5] Until recently, however, the majority of Cape Breton's residents and much of its income were dependent upon the coal and steel industries surrounding the city of Sydney in the southeastern corner of the island. Tourism promotions have not overlooked this industrial legacy completely. Treated as heritage as much as commerce, the industrial history of the colliery towns is part of the Cape Breton image. For example, the Cape Breton Tartan adopted in the early 1980s is a grey, green, and gold plaid symbolic of the island's green valleys, the light grey of Sydney's steel plant, the dark grey-black of coal, and the golden sunshine of an island surrounded by open sea. The island's anthem, *A Rock in the Stream*, a ballad by Rita MacNeil describes Cape Bretoners as survivors, first as immigrants and then as industrial laborers, all framed by the island's rural splendor. The company houses and railroad yards of industrial Cape Breton are part of its historical legacy, an example of the valiant struggles of Cape Bretoners against the forces of nature—a side trip from the scenic drive around the island.

Despite its reputation as the home of traditional Gaelic culture, Cape Breton has always been very much a part of a global economic system. Although the causeway to the island was built to bring in commerce, many islanders joke that it served better to take the island's children away to find work and home again for vacations and retirement. In the age of the Internet, the island is not remote—anyone can visit or leave the island through a number of websites in a matter of seconds. Cape Bretoners participate in the global economy as recipients of media and services transmitted from the metropolitan centers of North America but also as active members as they engage in strategies necessary to mediate changing economic conditions. Despite their reputation as traditional highlanders, Cape Breton residents are just as likely to hold graduate degrees as a fiddle or set of bagpipes.

While Atlantic Canada uses its "folk" traditions and geographic isolation as a draw for visitors, its struggling regional economy and distance from the global centers of North America place it on the edge in more ways than one. Within the Maritimes, Cape Breton and its neighboring island, Newfoundland, are considered the most marginal—socially, physically, and economically. At the time of my research, island comedians made joking references in skits and songs to "Cape Breton Barbarians" as a people who lack the modern sensibilities that define success in a progressive First World country. Cape Bretoners knew that mainlanders like the gas-station attendant and waitress mentioned above and those "away" in central Canada looked down upon them, and they made fun of themselves in return. They used the stereotypes of clannishness, fierceness, and creativity that characterize the highland lifestyle with self-deprecating pride. With a modern twist, the highland heritage of the eighteenth century was mixed with a derogatory critique of the twenty-first century welfare state. They joked about receiving the "pogie" (unemployment insurance) while at the same time strategizing about opportunities for their children.

Informal forms of wisdom such as knowledge about relationships within a community or local practices of communication are often discarded as "traditional" and unnecessary in translocal markets of the global economy. As residents of marginalized communities produce new ways of surviving in a deindustrialized world, two kinds of activities are emphasized: individual acquisition of educational credentials to try to compete in a wider marketplace and local community practices of collective survival. Economists often deride the latter, what Illich calls vernacular activities, as preventing development. Informal networks, however, help resist the creation of scarcity. More is not better, if more means less for someone else. Thus, vernacular activities do not prevent development so much as they challenge the economization of progress. For Cape Bretoners who buy into the economy of credentials, however, specialized skills have not yielded promised rewards in a rapidly changing labor market nor has the Maritime region benefited significantly from the education of its children. The brass ring of educational achievement and economic security remains elusive.

Living in Cape Breton
I lived in Glace Bay, Nova Scotia, during the summer of 1993 and returned the following year to stay for ten months. During this time, I conducted interviews with Glace Bay residents, including audiotaped life histories. My questions in all contexts focused on the story of education in the town, asking for personal and public histories. These questions resulted in conversations about many aspects of education and learning. While living in the town, I participated in formal and informal local activities. Perhaps more informative than interviews, participant observation allowed me to experience the everyday activities of the town.

Family stories and remembrances of my friends and neighbors were critical to my pursuit of the history of the area, especially for mining families. The mid-1990s were a difficult period for the town, and many of my friends and neighbors were worried about the future. They were quick to tell me, however, "It's when times are tough that you can see what Cape Bretoners are really like." My Glace Bay friends were truly warm and generous people even in times of sorrow. Conversations around the kitchen table, the backyard swing, and next door playing darts helped me get a grassroots perspective of the town; understand the names of neighborhoods and the relationships between families, occupations, and institutions; and grasp the pace of everyday life; and generally appreciate the good things that life has to offer in Glace Bay even in tough economic conditions.

The pure loquaciousness of Glace Bay people resulted in constant conversation. Conversations in Glace Bay had an interview-like character to them that made it possible for me to gather information in a variety of settings. Because of this local practice, my formal interviews were few and far between; instead, I learned to depend upon my ability to listen to the techniques of local talk, the interview that is conversation and the conversation that is interview. One informant commented on the Glace Bay style of discussion:

> I think we're great philosophers in Glace Bay but in an informal way. We can talk...you can see our philosophy that way. Just don't argue with the finer points of our philosophy.

Although my questioning of statements, arguments, and passing comments, trying to "unpack" expressions and gain deeper insight, were often met with irritation or humor, this type of sleeve-worn philosophy was helpful in gaining information. Other locations of public talk crucial to my research included meetings about labor, government, education, and development initiatives.

The ethnographic material presented in the following chapters is a result of sifting through interview transcripts, public documents, and publications, my field observations, and personal notes. The descriptions of Glace Bay, analysis of the economic conditions, and interpretations of education included in this text are my own narrative and should be read as such. Many of my friends in Glace Bay would nod in agreement at some statements but disagree with others. This is indicative not of misunderstandings on my part (although there are sure to be some of those as well) but of the diversity of interpretive positions within the town.

Quotations in the text are derived from interview transcripts and notes from interviews. In punctuating quotations derived from transcripts, I try to maintain the cadence of local speech patterns. This results in many sentences that are not questions ending with question marks. Cape Bretoners, especially women, often end their sentences in this way, similar to an Irish lilt. Some quotations are verbatim and others expanded from shorthand notes taken during conversations. When I could not be sure of the accurate phrasing or when an idea was expressed by a number of different individuals, I include paraphrased translations of the tone and substance of their comments. These comments are not set apart as quotations in the text. Individuals are not identified by name unless they hold public office or are well-known public figures. As a result, my introduction of "real" characters is rare. I hope, however, that the voices of the people of Glace Bay included here do not seem disembodied. Occasionally, when giving a case example of an individual story, I have used pseudonyms. These stories have also been altered slightly to protect anonymity.

Finally, I have chosen to write about Glace Bay in the past tense rather than using the convenience of the ethnographic present. Certainly, the town of Glace Bay still exists although it is now considered part of the Municipality of Cape Breton. The community has changed, however, since my visit despite the seemingly deterministic nature of the local economy. Fishing, the occupation that brought the first non-native settlers to Cape Breton's shores, and coal, the industry that created Glace Bay, are both gone as viable means of economic support, and yet many people stay and produce new ways to define their lives. Too much essentializing of the past has already occurred in this region, and I do not wish to contribute further to that calcification.

Organization of the Text
The community of Glace Bay hugs the coastline with a working harbor and neighborhoods of houses perched on the headlands overlooking the Atlantic. Clinging to the edge of a continent, the town struggled to survive. What was once "the biggest town in Canada" had approximately 19,500 residents in 1991 living in just over 6500 households. Unemployment rates in the town were around 25 percent and most young people planned on moving away from their homes and family. But Glace Bay was far from dead. In fact, residents defined themselves by their ability to survive and enjoy themselves in the process. To start any interview or conversation in Glace Bay as an outsider was to be introduced to the town's history through a series of conventional narratives and family anecdotes. These "creation narratives" are important to providing context for my discussions of education, community, and ideology. I start; therefore, in chapter 2 by introducing Glace Bay as a community in which the

past and present are understood as a system of contrasts and contradictions.

In chapter 3, I explore the ways in which the efficacy of education has evolved. When asked about education, specifically post-secondary education, townspeople often referred to school and training as distinct categories that implied external sources of information. Regardless of the program, university, college, or vocational school, any and all forms of formal education were considered "school." School implied a place in which one spent time in order to gain certification in a certain skill area. In further discussions of what it means to be educated and how education plays a role in the goals and aspirations for local residents, the term "education" was used as a reference to self-improvement or "getting ahead," referring to the possibilities that certification and knowledge acquisition might offer. Within a conversation about schooling and training, however, there were multiple references to the power of knowledge and learning as ideals for self-improvement and status attainment, not just skills acquisition.

Skills acquisition and retraining, however, are primary to the rhetoric of regional economic development. In chapter 4, the role of the state is introduced as a vital influence on both the reproductive and equalizing power of schooling. The role of government in providing access to that education was an important aspect of understanding education in Glace Bay. Local residents recognized the paradox of training for jobs that did not exist and yet continued to do so.

In chapter 5, I continue my discussion of the multiple definitions and contexts of education by looking more closely at local forms of literacy, empowerment, and practices of self-improvement. Conversations about training and schooling do not address more complex systems of learning and constructions of knowledge (utilitarian or otherwise) necessary for everyday living. Instead, the investigation of multiple definitions of literacy is required to examine the multiple ways in which people discover information, acquire skills, and educate one another for everyday survival. Personal knowledge, that which is gained in study (both formal and informal) or through dialogues outside the mainstream, may or may not fit into local conventions of conversation or "common sense." These elements of what was local or translocal with regard to knowledge were also important to issues of mobility within the town and away in terms of how knowledge was acquired and shared.

In the chapter 6, I return to my discussion of the productive possibilities of education as a form of self-improvement and community development. Education as a development strategy in Glace Bay has been contradicted by the lack of work available locally and the costs associated with acquiring credentials. In what ways did education provide positive rewards to local residents that might not have been acknowledged in a development model that focuses on vocational training for employment in existing but declining modes of production? In what ways has the commodification of educational credentials affected Glace Bay residents, and how might they turn this process to their benefit? What other forms of education and values for learning have been practiced in the town, and how might they lead to new forms of economic development which would enhance the survival of the community? In what ways can we see education as a productive process with transformative effects that go beyond vocational training or social reproduction? My goal is to find ways to allow the voices of these individuals living in an educated world to speak to the institutions which provide those credentials in a way that recognizes both the productive capacities of local learners as well as their educational needs.

Notes

1 Glace Bay residents voted on a number of occasions not to allow the community to become a city, and because of its sizable population Glace Bay was for some time the largest "town" in Canada.
2 French soldiers from the fortress at Louisbourg mined coal from the cliffs of Donkin for export as early as 1714 (Newton, 1992).
3 *Cape Breton Post*, September 19, 1922. It is not clear in these newspaper accounts whether the "college" mentioned was the existing extension office of St. Francis Xavier University (located in Antigonish) or if they planned on a labor college to grow out of the mechanical institute, which held night classes at the high school.
4 Canada's benevolent treatment of Cape Breton's Gaelic culture is unlike the assimilationist policies of the British government in Great Britain which made traditional Gaelic practices in Scotland, Ireland, and other Gaelic strongholds in the British Isles illegal.
5 The full-dress tartan or tailored costume with kilt, etc. is traditionally only worn by lairds or lords, not landless peoples. Highland families might have had claim to a tartan (in other words they had the right to wear it) but such garments were very expensive and not likely to be found on immigrants traveling in steerage to the New World (Dunn, 1991).

CHAPTER 2
"From the Bay"

> *We thought we were poorly treated boys*
> *When no dough for work was found,*
> *But many a briny tear was shed*
> *When the Pluck Me burned to the ground.*[1]
> —Men of the Deeps

Glace Bay was founded in 1901 as a company town, populated by immigrants recruited from Europe, the British Isles, Newfoundland, and rural Nova Scotia. The formation of the town of Glace Bay was, in many ways, similar to the creation of industrial towns throughout North America, full of contradictions "between the interests of the corporations and the communities that grew up with them" (Pappas, 1989). Like other colliery towns, the conditions for the early coal miners were severe and dangerous.[2]

> For many generations the history of coal mining was a sad chronicle of man's inhumanity to man, a continuing saga of exploitation, oppression, and persecution by companies motivated solely by greed and swollen profits built through the suffering of low-paid miners and disregard for even the most basic safety measures....Without leadership and organization, miners were doomed to a serflike existence, forced to live and work under intolerable conditions little short of slavery. (Mellor, 1983, p. xii)

In residents' stories, the coal industry acted as the economic force behind the incorporation of the town, the framework in which the town conceived of its past, and, in more negative terms because of the industry's decline, its present and future. In the Bay's collection of narratives, coal was not dead but king, a royal legacy as well as a brutal industry. Glace

Bay was founded on coal literally, as the town sits on miles and miles of underground mines running under its streets and houses.

This chapter explores the ways in which Glace Bay residents defined themselves and their community. This discussion is important because residents' conception of the past framed their decisions relative to their future. The historical consciousness with which people in the town narrativize their past helped establish issues that were shared in common, building a strong sense of community identity. These narratives also serve to raise questions regarding the politics of recognition within the town. What roles did institutions of power and of empowerment play both locally and "away"? What local practices of autonomy and efficacy within the nested contexts of family, neighborhood, community, and religion did individuals use to articulate their own strategies for self-improvement? How did the politics of difference, differences of class, ethnicity, race, and gender, affect educational practices and aspirations in Glace Bay?

Above the ground, to maintain or not maintain a sense of diversity in the town was a conscious choice. Although older residents talked about visible ethnic differences within the town and everyone acknowledged religious differences, explanations of the town's identity focused upon the communal heritage of the labor struggles and mining rather than the plurality of its immigrant population. By narrativizing this history, Glace Bay residents chose to imagine their past as a communal whole. The organizing issues for Glace Bay residents were both economic and social as they worked to build a sense of community from their varied backgrounds.

In an interview with a local minister, I asked how he would describe the community he serves. "Enduring," he said. I asked what he meant by that, and he said the people had taken a lot. Challenging him, I asked what the twenty-year-olds had endured, and he said he was talking more about the older people who had been through the deprivations of the mines. "The mines, you know," he went on, "they made this town, they are its heart." "What about the fishermen?" I asked in reply, and he responded that they were very important and rarely mentioned. "What about the merchants and small businesses?" I pressed, and he said, "Equally important!" So why, I asked, did he say that mining was the heart? "It's the way they present themselves," he said.

In talking about Glace Bay and its collective social identity, "the way they present themselves," I am, in essence, drawing a picture of the town most residents recognize and yet one in which many residents would argue they don't quite fit. In the same conversation that a mother might tell of the coal-mining strikes and struggles of the town, she might also tell of her brother's success as a mine official and her son's accomplishments as an engineer. Townspeople consistently identified with both the labor history of the town and the successful participation in management and professional occupations of their family members. What the community shared included that which was not held in common—pride in different kinds of achievements.

The unified way in which Glace Bay residents chose to remember their town was possible because Glace Bay as an imagined community, to use Anderson's (1983) now famous phrase, did have a shared history, one of struggle and performance which had produced generations of survivors. Anderson's notion of an imagined community refers to a national identity, but he notes that "all communities larger than primordial villages of face to face contact (and perhaps even these) are imagined" (p. 6). The imagined community of Glace Bay as a colliery town did not exclude membership in a larger national community because the collective narrative of the town was also a narrative of a Canadian town and as such Glace Bay residents were both local residents and citizens of a modern state. They clung to their identity as coal miners and as survivors even if they or members of their family had pursued other occupational paths. At the same time their pursuit of education and professional careers was made possible because of their rights as national citizens and members of a "First World economy."

Glace Bay residents and expatriates often made statements like "We're Cape Bretoners first, Canadian second, and Nova Scotian third—if we have to be." The local identity of Glace Bay residents as Cape Bretoners provided a "space" in which individuals' struggles to improve the conditions of their lives could be seen as successful relative to local standards. At the same time, they were also part of Canadian society and equally deserving of the rights of citizenship and opportunities afforded by that membership. During World War I and World War II, the large number of Glace Bay men who served in the trenches in Europe led to the expression, "Are you from the Bay, Boy?" (pronounced *bye*). The expression was brought home along with the wartime stories, and the nickname "Bay Boys" stuck. The coal miners of Cape Breton helped build the industrial nation of Canada through the harvesting of a valuable national resource and through fighting for its honor and values abroad.

Anderson (1983) remarks that the willingness to die for your country is a demonstration of the strength of the imagined community. Although the precarious state of the regional economy made Glace Bay a marginalized economy relative to other parts of Canada, Glace Bay residents were not marginalized by their local identity; in many ways, it connected and gave them ownership of a national story.

The state was an implicit but no less important part of Glace Bay's local and national identity because of the consistent role of government in the economy of the region. Although derogatory comments about and historical references to past conflicts with external authority included the federal government in Ottawa and the centers of economic power in Toronto and Montreal, the provincial government held a contentious position of being closer to home (and therefore more local) but at the same time more antagonistic (due in part to negative actions in the past). The federal government provided the funds to subsidize the coal industry when private owners wanted to sell out, supported the fishing industry's downsizing programs, and maintained social welfare programs in general. It was, in these roles, a great benefactor. In contrast, the provincial government had an historic role in supporting the company against the miners, and had provided less in the way of financial support over the years and more in the way of "rules"—policy mandates and procedural guidelines—which irritated and constrained local residents. These complicated relations of "us" versus "them" between Glace Bay residents and government agencies added to local interpretations of authority and dependency.

Although the Glace Bay creation story was an industrial one of a company town set in opposition to management who lived and made decisions away from the town, the success of many members of that community made such oppositions more ideological than political. Even so, conflicts between "us" and "them" continued to play an important role in the cultural logic of the town. The narrative told by Glace Bay residents about who they were as "Bay Boys" thus celebrated the creation of community and the contest between local autonomy and the dominant forces of capital outside—the company and later the government. Glace Bay residents' analysis and interpretation of their history, therefore, included an awareness of their role in the conditions of capitalism as both subordinate players and yet players nonetheless (sometimes even highly successful ones). As the conditions of that opposition between local autonomy and external capital declined, however, local residents had to find new ways to "imagine" their community. Strategies to capitalize upon their heritage as a company town in the form of explicit tourism campaigns and development projects further strengthen the notion that Glace Bay residents were aware of their modern national identity while constructing a local identity that celebrates a "shared" traditional heritage.

Black Around the Eyes: A History of Coal
Glace Bay's public memories of labor unrest reveal repeated references to survival, highlighting the conflict between local autonomy over the right to work and outside domination by the coal operators and the provincial government. In reaction to the disappointments and injustices of the mines and armed with activists who had immigrated from Scotland and England, Glace Bay became a center for labor activism. As a result, the first half of the town's one hundred–year–old history was full of conflict between "the company" and the people.

"Standing the Gaff" During the 1920s and 1930s, the town suffered harsh economic conditions because of the Depression, exacerbated by the continued low wages of the mines. Many of the stories residents told of this time period were of family members who left to find work in the Boston States and central Canada, following coal west to new jobs and more opportunity.[3] During the most famous of the mining strikes, the strike of 1924, the town survived the "gaff" (company lockout) for over a year. Threatened by the Nova Scotian government and, increasingly because of the perceived threat of violence, federal law enforcement, the townspeople bonded together to survive over fourteen months of almost total unemployment. Virtually every family has a story of how they, their grandparents, and/or great-grandparents survived this terrible hardship. One man recalled:

> The economy was terrible! Employment was mostly with the mines or the steel mills...then when the strikes came on, the company withdrew their services. The miners, since most of their money went into the company store, had to go to other merchants which wouldn't give them credit, so they were really in a bind. All the people on this street got kicked out of their houses. They had nowhere to go!

As the strikes of the 1920s and 1930s went on, help began to arrive from charitable organizations throughout North America. Truckloads of food and clothing eventually started arriving from sympathetic organizations in the United States and central Canada. National politicians spoke out against the Nova Scotian government for allowing such deplorable conditions to continue (MacEwan, 1976). Survival stories told by Glace Bay residents include stories of local merchants helping the miners, such as the Jewish grocer whose wife would hand out sandwiches to the striking miners' children on their way to school. Tales also included stories of how the local fishing and farming community provided fish scraps and greens for soup to help the miners' families survive. With assistance from church groups, the Salvation Army, the American Red Cross, neighbors, and their union, Glace Bay miners were able to "stand the gaff."

The establishment of decent pay, bearable working conditions, and a political voice for the working class in industrial Cape Breton was a long, hard time in coming. Even after the union gained recognition, the worst of the strikes were still to come. The operations of the mine and the company centered on the realization of profits and, because they would stand to gain a percentage of that profit, the provincial government supported those operations regardless of how inhumane they were. It was not until after World War II that the miners began to receive the compensation and working conditions that they had requested for so many years. Glace Bay is then a union town, one that prides itself on surviving the indignities and injustices of the company and provincial politics.

The survival stories did not include all Glace Bay families. Not every family suffered from the strikes, and not every miner was supportive of the early unions. There were numerous examples of ministers of a variety of denominations who spoke out against the strike and "godless strikers." Local papers of the time condemned the "red radicals." When describing personal histories, however, individuals called upon the public memories of a unified labor town, regardless of their family experiences. Even for those who were not dependent upon the company for wages, the town was so entrenched in the economics of coal that the labor history was shared. Despite fights between competing union organizations and ethnic and religious tensions, the shared story of the labor struggle created a common bond—a legacy of coal.

Modern Mining Following World War II, Glace Bay nurtured its role as a supplier of coal and men to the nation's war effort and national economic prosperity. Stories about the town during this period feature tales of civic boosterism and national pride. Local labor leaders had also, by this time, developed national affiliations. As Cape Bretoners and Canadians, the people of Glace Bay came to imagine themselves not as an isolated company town but as a part of modern Canada. In the 1950s, they literally became part of Canada as the government built a causeway to the island, connecting her to the mainland. The causeway made it easier for the island to play its role as part of "modern" Canada, but because of the increasing downsizing of island industries, local faith in the region's participation in the national economy began to falter. The causeway was considered by locals to function as a road away from the island, and the slow trickle of labor away from the island continued, never completely destroying the population but eroding it, like the sea erodes the coastal cliffs.[4]

The 1950s also brought changes—long-wall mining and public assistance. Some of the technology took away jobs, replacing manual labor with high-tech employment that required more education and formal apprenticeship training than in earlier years. Public assistance changed the face of the community, increasing the amount of government dependency on unemployment insurance and social assistance for some but also providing opportunities for higher education, government jobs, and a chance at the new middle class of a service-based economy for others. While some of these jobs were available in Glace Bay, by the late 1950s many people began to work in nearby Sydney, turning Glace Bay from a company town to a bedroom community.

During my interviews, I often commented on how there were very few detailed stories about the town after the World War II. Did nothing happen? The strikes of the first few decades of the town's history had all but ended because of the war effort and the relative prosperity of the postwar years. One man said, "Things were pretty good then. We were just going about our business." Despite the positive and patriotic spirit of the years following World War II and the advent of new mining technology, however, the coal industry declined in Cape Breton and never again reached peak production in terms of numbers of working miners. During the period after World War II through the 1960s, Dominion Steel and Coal Company (DOSCO) closed over half of the mines in town, while only developing two new mines.[5]

"Save Our Industry" By the late 1960s, although the overall population of the town remained over 20,000, there were fewer than 3,000 miners left in Glace Bay. They worked in mine number 26 near the neighborhood of New Aberdeen and Lingan located on Glace Bay's border with the town of New Waterford. The reduction in the number of miners was partly due to the switch to long-wall technology.[6] The conditions in the mine were still arduous, made only slightly easier by improvements in technology.

As the industry faltered, the unions became less and less antagonistic to the company and coordinated more of their efforts to make the mines as productive as possible. In the face of losing more jobs with more mine closings, the unions were in a difficult situation. Although the labor party (the New Democratic Party, or NDP) had won political seats in Cape Breton County, because they were not able to provide positive economic solutions for the troubled coal and steel industry, they rapidly lost public support. I questioned why the public would seem to turn from its labor roots, and one resident responded, "The unions are only a help when we're working. If we aren't workin', then nobody's happy."

With increased competition of global markets for coal, even modern technology could not guarantee the success of the mines. By the 1960s, the local economy showed no signs of improvement and became more and more dependent on government subsidization.[7] When DOSCO threatened to close the steel mill in Sydney in 1967, following the closing of most of the area mines, the people rallied in the streets to ask the government to "save our industry." In response to the public outcry and threat of violence, the Canadian government stepped in and created a crown corporation, Cape Breton Development Corporation (DEVCO), to replace DOSCO.[8] This period of the late 1960s was often referred to by local residents as the beginning of the end of Cape Breton industry. It was also the start, however, of a new era of government presence in Cape Breton. Despite the government intervention, the lack of real industrial growth on the island meant more emigration, especially of blue-collar workers, to the growing heavy industries of central Canada. By the end of the 1960s, the relationship between the government, in this case the Conservative party, and economic development projects was secured by the establishment of DEVCO.

The emphasis, during this period of economic development initiatives, was on the right of employment. Where they once fought the company for their right to work, with the change of ownership to the government, they continued to demand consistent employment. "Save our industry" was the rallying cry of the day. With the continued decline of the coal industry, miners and their families (albeit much more educated than before) continued to be vulnerable to external management and economic conditions. As they watched the coal industry gradually slip away from even the company's control, the townspeople turned their attention toward cooperation rather than contest with company management (now a government corporation). This was made easier by the fact that the "Company" now provided reasonable wages and working conditions. One man commented on the very different conditions for miners and their families in comparison with the "old days":

> The people who lived here didn't make even $50,000 in their whole life. The only time we ever got any money was when DEVCO took over. Now you make more money in a day than we did in a month.

The conflict between labor and capital so vivid in the image of families being turned out of company houses and starving during union strikes has less physical presence when those same families include trained engineers and their children are students at local universities or working for the government down the street. The dark industrial landscape of the early part of the century makes a more convincing backdrop to stories of inequality and injustice than neighborhoods full of cars, satellite dishes, and the occasional backyard pool.

Nash's (1989) work in Pittsfield, Massachusetts, describes this shift from workers' negative opposition to the company to an optimistic partnership with industry as indicative of the developing relations between the town and industry as unions and local merchants acquiesce to corporate demands for loyalty and the increased economic status of laborers in those industries. Although such partnerships might preserve currently existing jobs, Nash argues that viable economic diversification and local autonomy in decision-making are compromised. When the industry eventually goes, no amount of civic loyalty will save it. For Glace Bay, since the company was now the government, the continued presence of the coal industry in Cape Breton became a redistributive economic program of social support for the region. Rather than closing all of the mines (and the steel mill in Sydney) and forcing the region to find new sources of employment, the government subsidized coal and steel operations for more than thirty years to keep Cape Breton afloat.

One union leader described trying to motivate the men in the atmosphere of the declining industry. "For the industry to survive," he explained, "the ends have to justify the means." No matter how they tried, however, technological expenses and the high costs of safety measures in the mines did not allow coal to keep pace with oil and gas as primary fuels. "When the leadership says there's no use," he continued, "it trickles down to the men." In the spring of 1994, the federal government turned control of DEVCO over to regional management and, for the most part, discontinued financial subsidies. Some miners in the town spoke of this in positive terms as gaining more autonomy, saying things like, "Now we can finally run things right!" Yet most of the people with whom I spoke seemed to feel that this was just the final sign that the government had given up on the coal industry and them.

At the time of my fieldwork in 1994, the federal government weaned the subsidized crown corporation, DEVCO, off its subsidy, and centralized management was restructured. This allowed local control of the coalfields of Cape Breton for the first time in one hundred years, but long after the world's economy had lost interest in its production. The steel industry in Sydney was also on its last legs, waiting for foreign investors to buy out the crown corporation. That buyout never materialized, and by the winter of 2000 the government closed the steel mill. In the spring of 2001, DEVCO closed the last remaining coal mine in Cape Breton. Other government offices on which so many local people were dependent for social service jobs as well as financial assistance were also going through a process of reorganization and downsizing. Remaining strategic initiatives focused on tourism projects that bring tourists across the causeway to Cape Breton, but with no hotels or beautiful beaches, the colliery towns had little to offer them. The choice to stay, to work the mines or other industries, was all but gone.

Glace Bay Identity
By the mid-1990s, the physical presence of the mines in Glace Bay was muted. The stories of mining and of mining families all had a past-tense flavor. Perhaps, because the mines no longer played a primary role in the town's economy and everyday life—you no longer saw coal miners with their faces blackened walking down the street swinging their lunch pails—the collective identity of the community as a colliery town had become more nostalgic. With fewer than four hundred miners working in 1995 and no new training apprenticeships offered since 1982, coal min-

ing was no longer a viable career option for Glace Bay's children to consider. Although older residents and pensioners still called for the reopening of Donkin mine (never fully opened in the early 1980s) or the creation of new mines, the legacy of coal mining had a better chance of becoming a cultural relic of tourism promotion than returning to its former levels of production. While still contributing to the economy, coal mining as a historical example existed side by side with coal mining as a dying industry.

The primacy of coal mining to the town's sense of identity was made clear to me not through the published economic and labor histories of the town but through an angry exchange with a Glace Bay resident. A month or so before the end of my fieldwork, I was socializing with some neighbors when I realized one of their relatives, a coal miner, was glaring at me. I finally asked if something was bothering him, and he said, "You know what it is." I assured him I didn't and asked if he would tell me. After a half hour or so of trying to find out what I had done to offend the man, he finally said, "So, you don't think coal miners are important, do you?" I was surprised and asked what had made him think that I didn't. "You know what you said," was his response, and I was back where I started. Thinking carefully, I realized that he had probably heard, secondhand, some of the interview questions I had been asking around town and had probably heard reworked versions of comments I had made about my discoveries in those interviews. I asked him more questions, explaining more about my research and other interviews as I did.

In my conversations with people in town, I told him, I had noticed that the history of people and events not related to the mines was seldom told. I had asked people, in my interviews, if they thought the history of the coal mines had perhaps overshadowed other institutions and practices in the town, especially in light of the fact that it had been decades since the coal mines had employed the majority of workers or contributed significantly to the town's economy. I had struck a nerve. "Everything about this town is about coal," he yelled at me. "What do you mean that the miner is not important?" I assured him that I did think the miner's story was important, but I was also trying to understand the lives and stories of other people, people like his daughter who worked in a local business. "Those businesses wouldn't exist without the coal miner," he retorted. I agreed with him again. It was true that the town would not have been much more than a fishing village if it were not for coal mining.

This exchange haunted me for days. Had I underestimated the importance of coal mining? In retrospect, I realized that it was not my questioning of the importance of coal mining which had angered the miner but my insistence on a temporal history of the town which underplayed the relationships which he considered important to an understanding of what the town "is." To invoke the community of Glace Bay is to see the past not as a series of events (although the story does have a temporal aspect in terms of the sequence of strikes, of ownership, and of closings) but to claim "a memory of relations which no longer exist in real forms" (Greenhouse, Yngvesson, and Engel, 1994). Although it is true that coal mining no longer played the economic role in the town that it once did, this did not reduce the importance of the relations of coal mining to the identity of Glace Bay as a "colliery town."

Cape Bretoners All The narrative conventions of Glace Bay's creation myth leave little room for talking about differences within the town in direct terms, especially differences of ethnicity, religious faith, and gender. Solidarity was offered up for public consumption, similar to the way that Cape Breton tourism promotes the island as covered in a Gaelic swag of green, gold, and steel-gray tartan. Glace Bay residents, like their neighbors in rural Cape Breton, would prefer to talk of *ceilidhs* or parties around the kitchen table than the differences of those who pull up their chairs. Social conflicts caused by religious divisions between Catholic and non-Catholics or the various ethnic and racial backgrounds of the early miners were treated as friction that had been resolved with the passage of time.

As discussed earlier, workers and their families recruited by the company settled Glace Bay and other "coal towns." Italian, Ukrainian, Polish, Irish, Welsh, and English immigrants added to the town's dynamic growth. While these immigrants were not likely to go back to their country of origin, they were likely to follow the patterns of their Nova Scotia–born neighbors in following a two-way pipeline of labor traffic to and from the Atlantic provinces to the industrial regions of New England and central Canada. Again, individuals would network with family members and friends from "home" to find jobs and places to stay in "the Boston States" (the United States, particularly New England), Ontario, Alberta, and British Columbia. Many never returned to Cape Breton, but many of those that settled "away" maintained their island identity in the

Maritimes through relationships with extended family and visits to the island.

Glace Bay residents answered my questions regarding the diversity of ethnic groups in Glace Bay by referring to the solidarity of the miners. They told stories of the camaraderie and humor that characterized miners' relationships with one another. It was this camaraderie, they explained, that made it possible for them to all work together and which shaped their identity as Cape Bretoners, despite their ethnic, racial, or religious differences. To work together was not just a necessity of survival but an experience that allowed the miners to develop a sense of local identity and national pride:

> We no longer called them foreigners once they came to Cape Breton. There were so many Scots with the same name so there'd be a lot of nicknames, so when the foreigners or Newfoundlanders came in they'd be intermarrying and get names. They became Cape Breton. There was no such thing as foreigners. We made nicknames and then we were one big family. The Polish even learned to speak Gaelic perfect. Bilingualism, biculturalism. No one complained that we didn't have one language. We had to put up with all sorts of languages....Italians were particularly good at the accordion and the Scots were good at the bagpipe, and regardless of your nationality or politics they would socialize together.

This blurring of national origins and politics into a united front was also useful in the early labor struggles against the company.

When I realized there had been a variety of ethnic groups brought to Glace Bay by the company during the first few decades of the town's history, I asked a working miner how these ethnic groups maintained their identity in light of the prevalent Gaelic culture in the region. He shrugged and said, "Oh, it was so long ago, we just blend together now." Ethnic differences, although evident in family histories, were less recognized in Glace Bay's communal history.

Sterling: The Black Experience One of the most glaring differences not recognized in Glace Bay's public history was the racism that existed between the town's black and white residents. Although most Glace Bay neighborhoods generally held a mix of ethnicities because of the blending of immigrant groups around the mine heads, the one exception was the neighborhood of Sterling, located near the center of town behind the Sterling Shopping Center. Once home to over a hundred black families, by 1995 there was fewer than ten families still living in Glace Bay. Black families faced racism in school and on the job that overshadowed personal successes. MacLeod (1995) argues that the longer a family remains in an environment in which aspirations are not achieved, the more likely there is to be a leveling of expectations leading to reduced academic achievement. One of the black residents of the town who dropped out of school to work in the mines during the 1950s talked about his difficulties in the mines and his analysis of why many of the black youths in town did (and do) so poorly in school:

> I got my underground manager's papers but never got the opportunity. Then I got passed over a few times, and then when they did offer the job, I said no. They were looking for a fall guy, and by this time I had lost an eye and had the coal dust...in my lungs you know....It's like putting a flea in a jar. He'll hit his head for a while, but then he'll only jump so far. Even if you take off the cover, he'll only jump so far. You know you won't get any farther than that.

Although he tried everything he could, he said, his children did not do well in school and had not completed any of the training programs he tried to get them into. "It's not that they're lazy," he said, "God knows, I can tell laziness from hard work! It's just that they don't believe and I can't give them that." As bad as coal mining was, the old miner said, at least it was a sure thing. Without the "sure thing" of coal mining and in the face of open discrimination toward blacks identified by educators and social service workers in the town, the aspirations of young minorities did not match those of their white counterparts.

Fighting over God Despite the strong "spin" on solidarity in Glace Bay, Glace Bay residents were also quick to point out that the town had been divided between Catholic and non-Catholic since its inception. While miners may have set aside their differences in order to work together, above the ground town politics were divided on religious grounds. I often asked, in my interviews with Glace Bay residents, if there was a difference in economic class or professional status between the non-Catholic and Catholic communities. Many of my interview respondents felt strongly that while there was obviously a division along religious lines in the town, neither side benefited more than the other did:

> You see they're very fair about it. Once we have a Catholic mayor, we have to have a Protestant one. And then they would switch again. We'd never elect two mayors from one faith in a row!

Improvements made by town leaders upon existing schools and the building of new schools seemed to correlate with transitions from one mayor to the next and alternated between Catholic and Protestant facilities.

Other residents, however, insisted that the Protestant population had more economic and political power. Census figures for the town up to 1961 show the Catholic and non-Catholic populations to be of a relatively equal size. People in the town suggested that in the recent past the Protestant population had declined significantly more than the Catholic population. "The Protestant kids were more likely to leave and not come back," one man explained.[9] With the decline in church participation in all denominations and reduced political presence of the Catholic Church in the region, these changes were difficult to analyze.

Not Bay Boys Throughout the public history of Glace Bay's coal-mining past, the role of the miner's family, his wife, daughter, or niece was rarely mentioned except as long-suffering supporters of the industrial laborers. As discussed earlier, the life of the miner's family was difficult, especially during the early decades of the town's history. At one point in a historical documentary of the town shown at the Miner's Museum, the film shows still photos from the 1920s of the wives of miners and their families running to the deeps in answer to emergency sirens. The women were shown in a series of photographs running up over a rise surrounding the mine, silhouetted against the gray sky. The poignancy of this moment in the film was chilling in that a mine accident, even using modern mining techniques as the families of Westray, Nova Scotia, miners on the mainland can attest, almost always ends in fatalities. The film image of women running against the gray Atlantic sky was meant to give the audience a sense of the horror of waiting to hear who was caught in the accident, who was unaccounted for, and who would be grieving that night.[10] The film represented what was perceived to be the difficult life of a miner's wife and family, a life full of the constant dread of tragedy—a tragic story.

Women's participation in the town's history included far more complex roles than those depicted in the melodrama of the miner's wife; in many cases they acquired education and training to pursue active careers within the town and beyond. Besides teaching and nursing, women took jobs as stock clerks in local stores and learned bookkeeping and inventory skills that they would then apply to their family finances, helping to keep them afloat during the lean years. On-the-job training and professional programs were important to developing a sense of self separate from the role of wife and mother.

During a dinner conversation between two women from the neighborhood of New Aberdeen (both in their late sixties), the importance of personal autonomy, competence, and efficiency in the workplace was described as characteristic of women's work. One of the women described her job as a stock clerk in her early twenties:

> I was good at my job. I could keep most of the figures in my head, I always knew where the inventory was and could estimate what we would need to order even before the store owner. We had fun in those days, but we worked long hours. You see the miners worked in shifts, so we'd have to be ready for them and their wives would try to do their shopping in between preparing meals after those shifts. The long mine hours made our hours long too, but we were busy just trying to keep up with the pure volume of it all.

In response to my questions regarding the level of responsibility they were given in their jobs, they both responded enthusiastically. One said,

> They couldn't do without us. I took a business course in school and so I had the bookkeeping experience. I kept the books as well as keeping the shelves in order. When I got married, I kept the books for my family too. But I kept working even after my first baby came.

Although both of these women had only finished a grade nine education, they continually referred to their schooling as the foundation for their skill in the workplace. Their pride in their skills as working women was therefore tied not only to work experiences but also to the schooling that gave them the opportunities for increased responsibility on the job.

One of the important aspects of these examples of women's personal histories lies in their autonomy from the coal company. Although they were not independent businesswomen, neither were working women in Glace Bay under the direct control of the coal company. Even women who worked in the offices of Dominion Coal on Main Street (once employing over three hundred clerical workers) were not as prone to the vagaries of production as the men working in the mines were. Women's work, less "dirty" than that of the miners and steelworkers, was also less erratic. For families who learned that there would be no mine work, these noncompany or clerical jobs were often necessary. Women's stories of work, rather than projecting an image of the valiant and romantic miner, reflect the reality of unemployment throughout the history of the town and the importance of their contributions.

Gender plays an important part in the recognition and value placed upon types of work. This is played out in the way that, although women's occupations were an important part of household economic survival, the town was characterized primarily by its mining history. Part of this discrepancy was explained by the marginalization of women's public work by its feminine character. Women's roles in the public domain were feminized by their "cleanliness": the "pink-collar" activities of teaching, nursing, and clerical work relative to the "dirty" labor in the mines and on the sea. Work available to women that did include "dirty" labor, such as fish processing, held an ambivalent place in men's opinions as being undesirable due to its physical difficulty and assembly-line character. Women's work, therefore, was either feminized by the "clean" nature of their professions (which also raised negative connotations of being directly linked to the company or management) or lacked the creative autonomy of the room-and-pillar miner or independent fisherman. One exception to this was women's participation in the fishing industry where women worked as partners in the family business but often from their kitchen tables.[11]

Although many women worked outside the home, the demands of a family were a heavy responsibility but not usually openly acknowledged. Women's work both public and private was still perceived as secondary to men's, albeit dirtier, labor. The silent value of women's labor versus men's is important to understanding diversity among mining families. While the miners shared similar circumstances, the relative success of women in their economic strategies helps explain economic differences among families within mining neighborhoods. An older woman explained that it was the mother who acted as the strength of the family and that a lot depended on her:

> I know two families who lived in a company duplex. One side scrambled to make a living. Both fathers worked in the mine. The other side had teachers and nurses in the family and the other nothing. Nothing...they're beaten. Circumstances have beaten them. I think it's the mother in a lot of instances. What can a mother do with ten children? What can she do? She is beaten if she's not well. If she's a strong strapping women and she can face all this, all right. She'll survive.

Residents of Glace Bay often referred to family values as indicative of an individual's potential for success. Some went so far as to ascribe success or failure to the "strength" of a family's character. "They're weak stock" I was told about one family whose house was in disrepair and had a reputation for illegal activity. Although women's stories were rarely told as public narratives, residents considered the success or failure of women as important to the fate of their families.

Women's stories serve as a case example of the tensions economic mobility holds for all the residents in the town. While acquiring a white- or pink-collar job gives an individual better financial security than a job in a labor industry, it also separates that individual from the "folk" image of the coal-mining town. (Fishing families were accepted as maintaining a separate subcategory within the town, one that establishes links with other Maritime communities in which fishing was the primary industry.) For women, the role of the long-suffering support staff of the miner may have been less romantic than that of the heroes of the mines, but in pursuing education leading to professional careers in nursing, teaching, and clerical jobs, many women carved out the means for social mobility for themselves and their families. The unrecognized nature of women's work allows for this success to be overlooked in favor of the miners' story.

Women's stories serve as an important subtext to the narrative of a masculine, working-class town. The fierce loyalty residents hold for their local identity holds multiple dimensions, especially for women as they negotiate their identity within the contexts of domestic life and work outside the home. Women's roles in the family are instrumental in establishing their identity as Glace Bay community members, but their individual identities may be more sharply formed by education as a personal pursuit. Education's role in the mobility of individuals, whether taking a university degree west to find work or becoming a successful professional at home, is key to uncovering issues of class well hidden within the town. Education provides the means for individual mobility, to establish new identities within the framework of the town and without as individuals negotiate the borders of their professions and lives as members of learning communities.

The Politics of Class: "Us" and "Them"

Within the town, residents often framed differences, especially those of class, in an "us" versus "them" dichotomy. In interviews, I often heard people refer to difference in terms of "well, they do this" or "they do that." When I asked for clarification about who "they" are, the speaker often showed discomfort. For example, individuals who worked in social service positions were likely to use a derogatory expression like "welfare mothers" when referring to low-income families but rarely did so when referring to a particular person or even to a particular group within the town. It is important to keep in mind that although Glace Bay had a population of 19,500 in 1995, there were 6,690 independent households, many of which were familiar to one another (Statistics Canada, 1991). To talk negatively of a group was to perhaps include a relative or a neighbor; because of this, "they" were often defined as someone from "away" or someone who had taken on the unfamiliar characteristics of an outsider.[12] The above comment about a family being of "weak stock" was a slip, I believe, from what were normally very careful references.

As a result of chronic government dependency, some residents in Glace Bay disparaged the "abuses" of the welfare system by others. Residents of all ages and occupational groups (including the unemployed) spoke of "them" as residents of the town who were not conforming to what they believed was acceptable or respectable behavior. In this respect, "they" were acting like outsiders, people who did not embody Glace Bay norms of "scrappy" self-sufficiency. For example, while playing bingo at the Dominion Center I spoke with a group of older women who were lamenting the way "they" get away with being lazy. One woman nodded her head across the room at a table of younger women who were laughing loudly. "They've got money to play bingo but not to get off welfare," she said with disgust. Comments about the number of children born out of wedlock and abuses of drugs and alcohol also accompanied these kinds of "us" vs. "them" conversations, indicating that the root of the critique may have more to do with lifestyle choices than dependency upon a government check.

While speaking of difference in terms of exclusion (who "they" were) seemed to be difficult for Glace Bay residents, often defining "us" was equally hard. I asked one resident whether he felt there was a "local" identity in the town when he was growing up and what that was. He talked at length about the different national and international newspapers available when he was growing up and the ethnic diversity of the neighborhoods, but had difficulty explaining what it meant to be local:

> Well, it's difficult to know exactly how to put it. Because to me it was very cosmopolitan, I don't mean in the sense…I mean in the sense that with re-

ligious and ethnic differences and so on it was all there....But there was certainly a little world of our own, there's no question about that.

When I asked the same question of a young woman who had lived away in Ontario, she also had difficulty putting "us" into words. She said it was easier to describe coming home after living away and adjusting to local life again. She told me a story about how she had to readjust to the closeness of the community:

> There were different little things. Like I was shopping with my daughter and I remember waiting in line and this older man came up and picked her up. He was wearing a plaid shirt and rubber boots, you know...harmless, but still, I was very protective of my kids and I remember it was all I could do not to... And I remember he came over and picked her up and took her over and sat her up on the counter and started this talk, you know, "What a great little girl, what's your name, dear?" I was just having a fit. So anyway, that's where I still was. Now mind you, I've come a long way, to interact around here.

This mother's natural instinct to protect her child from a stranger was in direct conflict with the "stranger's" assumption of responsibility for a child of the community. Having gotten used to being careful while living away, she became aware of and had to get used to the assumptions of living at home. Defining what it means to be "from the Bay," what was "local" in terms of norms and expectations, was easier for those who had some experience away from Glace Bay, but that time away required readjusting to local ways of interaction upon return.

For Glace Bay residents, trying to describe increases in economic stratification between the employed and unemployed or other social changes often required using and reinforcing narrative constructions of the past. Living in renovated company houses built in the 1920s, for example, more affluent residents referred to the stories of the miners' struggles when describing their home, while pointing out their new deck or how they remodeled the bathroom to make way for a new hot tub. Of course, many of the old company houses in town had not received this kind of upgrading, but the differences between the economic resources of the people to do so (or not) were seldom acknowledged.

The lines between "us" and "them" drawn so distinctly between "local" and "non-local" during the miners' strikes were blurred in the context of the changing economy, emphasizing how these distinctions were derived from contradictions as well as consensus. Practices of "leveling," which had traditionally served local residents well in maintaining a local identity in opposition to an external authority, were less viable, in some ways, in a knowledge economy. The myth of community was, in part, based on the notion of a level playing field for all residents through the tools of experience and education. In this sense, Glace Bay residents believed in the egalitarian principles of a meritocracy. With the rising difference between the haves and have-nots caused by deindustrialization and unemployment, however, this equal footing was lost.

"Makin' It" An unspoken part of these story lines of what it meant to be from Glace Bay was the relative success of some families. As one of the retired miners quoted earlier said, "Now you make more money in a day than we did in a month." Pensioners, a term used for both miners collecting union pensions and adults receiving Canada Pension, the Canadian equivalent of Social Security and/or disability payments, also received consistent incomes. In addition, the "boom years" of relative prosperity during the 1950s and 1960s resulted in more jobs outside of the mine with decent salaries. The traditional story of a colliery town does not include the success of professional miners holding engineering degrees or of the children of miners who pursued other occupations. Glace Bay residents have had success stories separate in many ways from the tale of the rise and fall of the mining industry.

The Glace Bay "folk" identity, which idealizes its working-class heritage, was very strong. Even attempts to physically "create" middle-class structures in Glace Bay met with mixed results. In the late 1970s, they began building a subdivision called Tanglewood about five minutes from Glace Bay on the Sydney highway and convenient to individuals working in Sydney. It was supposed to be middle-class housing reflecting the growing character of Glace Bay as a bedroom community to Sydney, but no one seemed to be interested; the subdivision never really took off. Only one of five planned communities was completed, and it gained a neighborhood name of its own. It was not Glace Bay and it was not Sydney; it was just Tanglewood. Instead of building new subdivisions, the practice of building larger homes in the backyards of older structures or renovating company houses in older neighborhoods allowed Glace Bay residents to participate in middle-class consumerism while also maintaining their identity and pride as people from "the Bay."

Quality of life in Glace Bay did, in many ways, reflect the simple character of a traditional "folk." With few liabilities, close-knit extended families, a strong commitment to self-sufficiency, and, ironically due to the weak labor market, a large amount of free time, the residents of Glace Bay enjoyed a relatively laid-back existence. Middle-class consumerism—pools, new decks, cars, summer bungalows, and recreation "toys" (snowmobiles and ATVs)—was easily absorbed into this laid-back character as long as differences between neighbors' economic standing were downplayed. Rather than striving for visible middle-class status, economic success was framed within the traditional social structures of the town—family, friends, and neighbors. The overabundance of skilled labor: electricians, plumbers, carpenters, etc., made home improvements easy to contract and, through bartering systems, easy to pay for. Even with an informal service economy, however, over 25 percent of houses in the town were in need of major repair (Statistics Canada, 1991), implying that some households did not have the resources or desire to improve their living conditions.

The Glace Bay "folk" identity was created by those living in the town, expatriates living away, and by those who returned home. Shared experiences, therefore, were less likely to add to an interpretation of local identity than shared desires for what the place might be. Regardless of social class, economic status, or educational credentials, Glace Bay residents and expatriates shared the desire to remember and "see" Glace Bay as a good place to be or to be "from." This required not seeing divisions within the town, especially of class, which might disturb the traditional "folk" identity they maintained or nurtured while away.

The image of Glace Bay as a unified whole reveals little about the everyday activities of the town's residents and the ambiguities of their lives. How did these ambiguities reveal multiple interpretations of the future for both individuals and the community? Like most of North America, community myths of solidarity require the integration of a variety of immigrant stories, a process of melding different national origins, faiths, and cultural values into a "shared" whole within which individuals can go about their everyday business (Greenhouse, Yngvesson, and Engel, 1994). This process often includes but frequently obscures contradictory interpretations of "the way things are." Although some differences, such as national origin, can be subsumed within a new regional identity, other contrasts, especially those related to economic status, must be continually negotiated. Social class, in particular, becomes a highly ambiguous category, especially with regard to the strong labor heritage of the town that is marketed to outsiders.

Critics of democratic systems of education claim that open institutions such as community colleges divert low-income and minority students from upper-level professional degree programs, thus reproducing social stratification (Brint and Karabel, 1989; Dougherty, 1994). What effect, if any, did Glace Bay's ambiguity regarding economic class have on this sorting of students? When and how did families that started out as immigrants, coal miners, and fishermen start to distinguish themselves, and what role did education play in that differentiation? The following chapter will address these questions, examining how the value of education evolved in Glace Bay.

Notes

1 "Pluck Me" stores were company stores named after the "plucking" the company would perform on the workers wages.
2 See Anthony F. Wallace's (1981) *St. Clair: A Nineteenth-Century Coal Town's Experience with a Disaster-Prone Industry* for an excellent description of the dangers of early mining techniques.
3 The "Boston States" is an antiquated phrase still used when referring to the United States, especially New England.
4 The town of Glace Bay sits on the edge of cliffs overlooking the Atlantic. During my research, its easternmost street was closed due to the erosion of the cliffs beneath it.
5 In 1894, Dominion Coal Company, founded by H.M. Whitney of Boston, was given the exclusive rights to Nova Scotia's coal resources for ninety-nine years. In 1920, Dominion, along with its sister company, Dominion Steel that owned and managed the steel mill in Sydney, and fourteen other companies were incorporated as British Empire Steel Corporation (BESCO). BESCO was reorganized in 1928 as Dominion Steel and Coal Corporation (DOSCO) (MacEwan, 1976).
6 A form of mining using hydraulic systems and cutting machines rather than manual labor.
7 "Government" in this case refers to the Progressive Conservative Party, which spearheaded this investment. In an effort to diversify the industrial base in the region, the government financed a heavy-water plant on the west side of Glace Bay. The project was slated to provide many jobs and another market for coal, but, like many development initiatives of this era, the plant never went into production. The labor party, National Democratic Party (NDP), was supposedly pushed out of power by these financial investments (MacEwan, 1976 see especially chapters 21 and 22).
8 Both the coal and steel industries were seriously in debt to the federal government before this transition. The grant of loans was a hotly contested political debate for years.
9 Of the non-Catholic residents in the town, the largest population decline was among the Jewish community. At the time of my fieldwork, the synagogue had closed, and there were no longer enough members to hold services in town.

10 The footage itself, however, may not actually even be of Glace Bay women. The curator of the museum commented, when I asked about the film, that in some instances film footage from mining regions of Wales and England had been used to supplement local material.
11 Family participation in the coal or fishing industries tended to be exclusive. Although there was some interchange between the two, the children of coal miners rarely went to sea and vice versa. Members of either group, however, might find work in business or in industries outside of Glace Bay.
12 Handelman (1982) describes such "concealment and revelation" as important to maintaining the "moral correctness of everyday social order" in isolated communities.

CHAPTER 3
"No Burden to Carry"

Most ethnographies of schooling in working-class or low-income communities focus on the question of social reproduction. Why is there a tendency for working-class children to end up in working-class jobs? Resistance theories help us understand why and how resistive practices reproduce social inequalities, but what of those individuals who work within the system, achieving the educational credentials supposedly needed for economic mobility, and yet fail to produce successful outcomes? What happens when individuals play by "the rules" and yet do not succeed?

In Paul Willis's (1977) landmark study, *Learning to Labor*, a group of working-class boys creatively resist the ideology of school by insisting upon their own cultural identity as opposed to that of the middle-class values of society. They act out in school, getting into trouble, and establishing themselves as "lads" similar in many ways to their working-class fathers. In contrast, the majority of the students in Willis's study conform to school values and go along with the success ideology of working hard within the prescribed system. What happens to these "good students"? Glace Bay students were much more likely to resemble this second group of strivers than the resisters even though they were also loyal to a strong local identity. Resistance theory, while helping to explain the cultural logic of subcultures which do not conform, does little to help explain the subjectivities of groups that do play by the rules and yet do not quite "make it" either.

Willis attributes the failure of the students in his study, compliant or deviant, to the deterministic constraints of the class structure in which the boys live although interpreted through the cultural milieu of the boys' lives. Bourdieu (1977) might call their failure a lack of cultural capital. In Glace Bay, however, most local residents were aware of what it takes to succeed. They had family and friends who were successful. It is therefore difficult to argue that their lack of success was determined by their status within the community or cultural capital. The blurring of class distinctions within the town made regional inequalities more acute than economic disparities.

More recently, Jay MacLeod's (1995) work, *Ain't No Makin' It*, examines the aspirations of two groups of inner-city teenagers. Using Bourdieu's concept of "habitus," he explains how structural factors of family, work, and school influence the ways that the boys make meaning of their lives and the aspirations they hold for their futures. While one group of teens resists authority in order to maintain their sense of cultural pride, the other group accepts the achievement ideology that if you try hard, you will succeed, and yet they rarely do. While the two groups of boys interpret their world differently, the result is still the same: Both groups fail with regard to their aspirations and expectations.

MacLeod's discussion of aspirations is important to exploring the reasons economic reproduction (the condition of being somewhat "stuck" in an industrial model) persists in towns like Glace Bay and why many residents were not as successful as they had imagined themselves to be. MacLeod argues that aspirations are tempered by experience, both of the individual and those around her or him. In Glace Bay there were consistent examples of both success and failure. The number of successful individuals from every neighborhood supported belief in an achievement ideology.[1] For example, class or gender did not seem to be a factor when a girl from the "wrong side of the tracks" could make it just as well as a boy from the more affluent neighborhood. In fact, the two might have dated while at university in Halifax. Unlike MacLeod's study, however, where the boys who believed in the achievement ideology blamed themselves when they failed, in Glace Bay unemployment and underemployment were often seen as predetermining factors, products of an economic situation that individuals were helpless to control. To challenge that economic model, to take risks with how they perceived themselves in it (by starting a small business for example or training in a nontechnical, nonservice field), was uncommon.

Resistance theory, therefore, does not help explain why individuals do not succeed when they have accepted the ideologies of achievement supported by a credentialing society. It does explain the actions of those who resist the status quo, but it does not work for an entire region of unemployed and underemployed individuals. Regionalized economies may offer another perspective on the problem of how to explain social reproduction of the strivers in neighborhood studies. That Glace Bay suffered from economic problems determined by outside forces is true, but Glace Bay residents were not victims. Through their interpretations of personal experiences, constraints, and opportunities, they both produced and reflected the world in which they lived.

Throughout my interviews in Glace Bay I heard residents, especially older miners, use the expression "it's no burden to carry" to refer to the value of education. "Getting your papers" or seeking out knowledge was a reasonable activity, adding value without (at least in theory) expense. They responded with this phrase when I asked about why miners would choose to attend mining school at night after working in the deeps all day or why nurses might attend workshops on teaching home economics to cooperative groups—two examples from the educational history of the town. Whether for credentials or self-improvement, the benefits of education to the individual were described as outweighing the costs. As requirements for educational credentials have risen, however, the "burden" of education in terms of its costs and return on investment has changed. The purpose of this chapter is to consider the ways in which the ideology of success in Glace Bay has been interpreted with regard to schooling as a means for self-improvement. How has the efficacy of schooling changed over time and how did these changes affect community values of education?

Popular Education

On more than one occasion, older residents of the town, especially pensioners, made comments about how a university education had been out of reach for the children of the miners. A local politician, a former miner who left the mines in the late seventies and went into politics, stated that "miners' sons didn't go to university." Although it was clear from the educational histories of a number of mining families that miners' children did indeed go to university, these types of comments indicated a conflict between success ideology rhetoric, which promotes working hard within the credentialing system, and the rhetoric of the labor movement, which promotes education as a tool to "fight" the status quo.[2] Who did go to college during the 1930s and 1940s and what were the alternatives if they did not?

Reading and Self-Improvement Through newspaper accounts and biographical information regarding the early labor movement in Glace Bay, it was clear that labor leaders saw education as a primary goal for the empowerment of the miners. Mellor (1983) writes of the importance of education to the labor movement:

> As each generation of miners succeeded the other, they learned that work stoppages and slowdowns were but poor weapons at best, and that political representation through the election of workingmen was the only sure method of redressing their grievances and improving their miserable lot in life. But to their consternation, they found the path blocked by a lack of formal education....Without formal education they were putty in the hands of unscrupulous coal operators. (p. xii)

According to published accounts, labor leaders, especially J. B. McLachlan, advocated the development of local publishing in the form of newspapers and pamphlets so that the people could inform themselves and gain power through knowledge. McLachlan also argued for a people's college that would provide a forum for the enlightenment of each for the betterment of all.

Although the individuals I interviewed did not personally participate in any such college, they did talk at length about the popularity of reading for the people of Glace Bay. As the subject of knowledge and knowing came up so often in my interviews, I began to ask my interview respondents when they first remembered learning something important, who taught them and in what contexts. Over and over, when asked the circumstances under which my informants first remember learning, they recalled learning to read and the importance of reading. The importance of family literacy to individual success in school is well documented; therefore, the value of reading in a household and in a community is a strong indicator of the cultural capital needed to successfully negotiate the field of formal education. After a while, I began asking the question "Was he or she a reader?" of each family member mentioned to try to gain a better understanding of just how widespread the practice of reading had been in Glace Bay families. Some talked about shelves and shelves of books, but most recalled sharing reading materials through public libraries and social networks.

In their recollections of the "boom years" of Glace Bay just prior to and after World War II, residents proudly told me of the number of bookstores the town once held (at one point as many as three) and their library. Wallace (1981) describes a similar build-up in the mining town of St. Clair, Pennsylvania, but attributes it solely to the rise of the middle class in that town. Although the desire for and consumption of information did not seem to be restricted to any one economic group, this pressure for the establishment of lending libraries and bookstores may be one of the first acts of the rising middle class in the town otherwise constrained by the external ownership of other forms of production. The egalitarian politics of the labor and cooperative movements would have spread the benefits of such practices broadly across families. Thus the pursuit of reading as a practice of self-improvement supported both community development in the form of sharing resources and individual self-improvement in the acquisition of skills that would be valuable in formal educational settings.

One woman from Paschendaele (the neighborhood surrounding the No. 11 mine which closed in 1913) explained that although her family had very little money, they were able to gain access to books through the local YMCA and local bookstores, some of which were newspaper shops which carried books and others full-fledged booksellers. Another woman in her sixties remembered a kind of ad hoc lending library in one store where the owner left used books to be borrowed and returned:

> We had a Thompson Sutherland Building on Commercial Street. It was one of those big square buildings two stories high and flat roof. And this side of it about twelve feet from front to back, was Charlie MacLeod's bookstore and he had all the papers and regular things, but on this side of the store [gesturing with her hands] all the way down he collected old books he could find and he stacked them on the shelves and you could go in there and take one and read it and bring it back for someone else to read. He never charged you a thing!

The public library of Glace Bay was founded in 1944, providing a public source for what had previously been a private or organizational supply of reading material. Fanny Cohen, a retired teacher who was instrumental in starting the library, described her strategies for getting books:

> I'm a mystery fiend. I've changed over the years too. Of course when the library opened, I read everything. My dear, and before there was a library, people borrowed books from one another. That's how I read too. I didn't

have the money to buy books! We did have a bookstore, but I was a member of a book club for a long time.

In the middle of the last century, more so than in today's world of TV and the Internet, local bookstores carried international and national newspapers in addition to local publications. These papers included weeklies from Philadelphia, New York, Toronto, and London. A retired teacher in his sixties spoke nostalgically about being able to get the sports scores and write-up of sporting events from any city in North America the next day! There were also as many as three local papers during the first fifty years of Glace Bay's existence, some sponsored by the labor movement but most the result of local publishing endeavors as a marker of a "civilized" town. As of the 1990s, there remained a weekly paper published in Glace Bay, *The Coastal Courier*, but the daily paper, *The Cape Breton Post*, was published in Sydney.

Although reading is not a gender-specific activity, most people reported the mother as the more likely parent to introduce reading to her children. Mothers were also more often identified by my informants as being the parent most likely to push her children toward higher levels of schooling. Because the mines had acted as a threat as well as a source of income for women and their families, education and training opportunities outside of mining were encouraged and suggested by mothers more than fathers. Most of the people I talked to reported that they had learned to read their ABC's at home, before attending school and that their mothers or grandmothers were usually their first teachers.

One woman talked about the shared nature of reading practices and how women would network in small clubs. These gatherings provided the opportunity to socialize but also to share what they had learned:

> This town was inundated with clubs. They had little money so they would pay some small dues, like a Christmas Club account really, and they had their clubs in their houses. I remember the children at school telling me, "Miss, tomorrow night is club night and it's in our house!" They weren't allowed to touch this or that and the house was cleaned up. The mothers went out once a week. It was a social upheaval. Oh yes, and then those who liked to read would mention it. "Have you read this, have you read that?...If you haven't got it, I'll loan it to you." And they always subscribed to magazines if they could afford them.

I asked if these clubs were important to the ways that people shared knowledge in the town as well as providing an opportunity to socialize. She responded,

> This seems to me to be the type of learning that actually maintains and is maintained within the community. It doesn't get taken away like training with the children. This is community stuff!

Other women fondly remembered book clubs, and some mentioned that they still subscribe to book clubs for their grandchildren. Although resources were scarce within the town, these were examples of the light load that learning carried in the pursuit of knowledge. Reading, an important learning experience that translates directly and well to formal educational settings, was supported by Glace Bay families across neighborhoods and economic situations. This emphasis on reading throughout the town in the early part of the century was echoed in the commitment to the building and support of schools, despite the limited means of the town's residents.

Reading, although associated with schools because of its importance in the school curriculum, was also referred to as a pleasurable activity. When I asked one man why he liked to read (his preference was the history of the Maritimes, especially Newfoundland), he said, "I guess it's like looking into a fire. You can lose yourself in it." Reading has often been studied as a form of escapist entertainment, but the pure volume of books in all kinds of homes in Glace Bay indicated not just an escape into fiction but a love of both the story and the knowledge it can reveal (Radway, 1984).[3]

Another older man whose mother had grown up in Gabarus, a small town southwest of Glace Bay, spoke of there being "a lot of reading in the country." "My grandmother and grandfather in the country read a lot," he said. "There were very few people that you'd meet that couldn't read." He had his own explanation for this in that "Country life was lonely, you know, not like life in town. They were smart people. Not all that smart in school learning, but smart enough." Reading is also identified as a "country" practice, which may explain why it was so widespread in the town as part of the heritage of those families who moved to Glace Bay from the outlying areas.

"Getting Your Papers" Vocational training, while not as useful for political liberation as literacy practices and labor education, was also emphasized in early Glace Bay history for its economic value. For most of its history, the pursuit of skills for employment was supported in Glace Bay by opportunities for on-the-job training resulting in a preference for experience over the "school learning" acquired in post-secondary training programs. Most of the occupations in town, including women's professions of nursing and teaching, could be pursued with the appropriate high school training and on-the-job experience. Most employers offered night school or apprenticeship programs by which individuals could move up their respective occupational ladders. "Mining school" for example, was available at night for those who wished to get their "papers." An admiring article in the *Sydney Post-Record* read:

> These mining classes provide a means for young men of the mines, qualifying themselves for any position in the mines up to manager and the cost is a mere trifle. (October 20, 1931)

Trade schools and "mechanics institutes" provided the means of furthering one's education and acquiring credentials for economic advancement. Newspaper reports and editorials from this period frequently discuss the need for "modern" education and training for the young people of the town. For example, in 1938, the local paper described an apprenticeship program as highly successful not only in training the participants but in creating new jobs:

> The most striking feature of the project locally has been the enthusiasm with which the young men tackled the training problem. Of the seventy youths in the program, great care has been taken in matching placement and interest. ...Some are so successful they are bringing in work for their employers. (October 26, 1938, *Sydney Post-Record*)

Most occupations in the town during the first half of the town's history did not require university educational credentials, and comments regarding a "modern" education usually focused on the practical attributes of training and the development of technology. Vocational training could provide increases in wages without changing a person's social status. In fact, getting your papers or management certification was often perceived negatively. Becoming a shift foreman or "overman" might mean entering a status position within the mine that would separate you from your friends, cousins, and immediate family; therefore, the pursuit of training must have had value beyond increased status, especially for men. For example, one man explained his decision to go to mining school in the late 1940s despite his lack of ambition:

> Yeah, I went to the classes because I was curious. I'm always curious; I want to know how things work. I'm always reading or looking things up...they [friends] come to me when they want to know the answer....But I didn't take the job, I didn't want to be management you see. It's OK for some but not for me.

Long after the strikes of the 1920s and 1930s were over, Glace Bay workers still considered management suspect, and some men would refuse promotions in order to avoid a substantial change in their social status. In the example above, training was a source of information as much as a path for economic advancement. The acquisition of knowledge had social benefits, as the individual becomes more knowledgeable—as indicated in the comment, "they come to me." In discussing education and training therefore, differences in definitions regarding useful knowledge and gaining credentials for advancement were important.

It is not clear how much (or how little) mining families aspired to university education prior to the Second World War. Graduation records and college attendance information were either destroyed or lost when schools were consolidated. In interviews with seniors who grew up during this period, however, I was told story after story of the sacrifices families would make to send at least one child on to further schooling. These stories confirmed the economic value of education more so than political rhetoric of the time regarding the empowerment of the miner (Mellor, 1983). Post-secondary education meant acquiring the credentials to get out of the mines completely—something most parents wanted for their boys. Realistically, however, for most Glace Bay residents in the prewar years, an elite university education would not be very useful if you wanted to stay in Glace Bay unless that training was in medicine or education.

The Cooperative Movement Although most of the educational opportunities in the region prior to and just after World War II were in trades training and much of the emphasis was popular or vocational education, post-secondary institutions also had a substantial presence. Institutions, especially St. Francis Xavier University (St. FX), initiated adult education programs, extension services, and the early stages of professional training for nurses and teachers. St. FX and other Catholic institutions, in particular, played a major part in bringing economic and social reform to industrial Cape Breton not only by participating in the growth of the public school services in the town but also in the form of adult education. The most famous example of this was the Antigonish Movement, an international extension program of St. FX. Through the Antigonish Movement, cooperative economic practices and education were stressed as ways to raise Cape Breton communities out of poverty by teaching the residents to work together. The Antigonish Movement served fishing villages as well as industrial Cape Breton and also sent extension workers to foreign countries. Addressing conditions of poverty as well as oppressive industrial conditions, the Antigonish Movement emphasized a liberation theology which promoted the empowerment of impoverished peoples to better their communities.

Ida Delaney, a current resident of Glace Bay, remembers working in the St. FX extension offices in Glace Bay during the late 1930s:

> The people were so poor, they could see the results quickly...they had a lot of curiosity. They also latched onto easy ideas...like five cents a week into the credit union. And the men in the study groups...they got a hold of the ideas, like the histories of the Charters and the Scottish populist movement. They took to reading so quickly...they knew it would make their lives better.

Women were also included in this educational movement through women's study groups emphasizing home economics and health care services. As a legacy of the Antigonish Movement, St. FX continues to be well known for its programs in adult education and social service.

Thus, popular education through reading, on-the-job training, or cooperative education provided a backdrop to the aspirations of later generations in Glace Bay. Not resistant to formal education, early Glace Bay residents pursued an array of learning opportunities, seeking knowledge that was both useful and entertaining. Educational aspirations were guided by the desire to "make it" in the industrial economy of mining and steel production and their attendant services including the newly professionalized fields of nursing, education, and business. Post-secondary education provided access to technology and professional development that answered local values for self-improvement and vocational ambitions.

Going to University: Higher Education in Glace Bay

The difference between extension services, professional training programs, and a full university degree program was significant. Knowing that a degree from St. FX, Dalhousie, or the University of Toronto was possible for only a few of Glace Bay's children, public schools, trade schools, and popular education remained the primary focus for most residents in the town through the 1950s. This would change, however, as universities became more open to serving a "professional" clientele rather than an elite and as educational credentials became more and more necessary for economic and social success.

The Modern University At the time of the formation of Glace Bay in 1901, fundamental changes were occurring in Canadian universities regarding the nature of knowledge itself. The needs of the new nation required "...greater relevance in a complex world now inhabited by the visible poor and the struggling immigrant" (Axelrod, 1989, p. xiv). Company towns like Glace Bay, full of immigrants recruited by the British Empire Steel and Coal Company (BESCO) and later Dominion Steel and Coal Corporation (DOSCO), were a perfect example of these new national issues. Changes in the economic structure of Canadian society also placed a new emphasis on educational specialization leading to "a culture of professionalism" similar to that evolving in the United States (Bledstein, 1976). Canadian higher education had followed a model that married a British system of "sponsored mobility" based on a rigid class system and the American "contest model" of meritocratic advancement. Because of this, Canadian higher education had consistently been more open than that of the British but less so than in the United States (Lipset, 1989).

The result of these shifts for towns like Glace Bay was a postsecondary system that, while still maintaining a certain elitism sponsored by traditional class bias, sought to extend its services to the needs of clients from all economic situations. Educational choices in Glace Bay after compulsory education were less class based (due to the lack of an established elite) than influenced by religious divisions between Catholics and Protestants. Religious difference was indeed a dominant discourse in Glace Bay. Unlike regions of North America and Europe in which discriminatory social institutions excluded Catholics from avenues of social and economic advancement, the strong presence of St. FX through its extension programs made separate but equally competitive educational opportunities available for Catholic students in Cape Breton.

Following World War II, the credentials necessary for economic success increased. With this increase, access to post-secondary education became an important issue for Glace Bay residents. Prior to the establishment of the University College of Cape Breton (UCCB), a small percentage of each graduating class from Glace Bay schools attended university.[4] The following table shows levels of educational achievement in Glace Bay following World War II.

Table 1: Educational Achievement in Glace Bay

Level of Schooling	1951	1961	1971	1981
Total Population	25,586	24,186	22,449	21,295
Finished none	866	605	0	0
Elementary	8,244	6,488	6,190	4,120
Secondary	5,687	6,847	6,605	6,930
Post-secondary	626	499	1,075	1,061

Church schools and the early public schools of Glace Bay provided basic education for the town. To pursue further education, students had to travel to universities off-island or enter training programs through trade schools or on-the-job apprenticeships.[5] With the success of each generation, more and more Glace Bay families sent their children to pursue post-secondary opportunities using new programs of financial aid and civic scholarships funded by these successful alumni.

Alma Mater Religious affiliation profoundly influenced strategies for post-secondary achievement in the postwar era. Students at St. Anne's High School might go on to St. FX in Antigonish or St. FX Junior College in Sydney; students at Morrison Glace Bay High School might go on to Dalhousie, Mount Alison, or Acadia (all Protestant schools). The educational ladder of success was very clearly defined. If they or their parents could not afford the tuition (and many could not), the universities often provided scholarships and work-study programs that made the experience possible.

This patronage was supported by a strong alumni presence in the town. St. FX had the largest single alumni presence in the town because of the institution's strong commitment to Cape Breton students.[6] Protestant students were recruited by Mount Alison, Dalhousie, and Acadia, institutions with graduates represented in the town's leadership, themselves the children of immigrant miners. A retired teacher and son of a miner described how he was told by a leader in one of the town's civic organizations after taking his final exams that he was "ready to go." He learned that his tuition had been paid and that a part-time job was waiting for him in Halifax to help defray his living expenses. "I didn't even ask for the help," he exclaimed.

"The Teacher Mill of Canada" Women graduating from high school in the 1930s and 1940s were often more likely than men to continue their education due to increases in professionalization in nursing and teaching and the growth of proprietary schools for business. One retired nurse spoke proudly of her education and her family: "When you went to college in the forties," she began, "it was a big deal! My mother stood on the step of the house and cried!" She went on to talk about how important it had been to her to "get out" of Glace Bay. "I couldn't wait! To get away from this close-knit clannishness." She spoke both fondly and with bitterness about the closeness of her family and those of her neighbors. She explained that what she called clannishness extended beyond the Scottish families that made up the largest ethnic group in the town and reduced the antagonism that might have existed between ethnic and religious groups. "It helped us survive," she exclaimed. "We knew too much to ignore each other's pain."

When I asked how common her kind of education would have been for her generation, the woman clapped her hands and exclaimed, "My parents lived for three things: food, shelter, and education!" Family values for education often followed ethnic lines, but because of the intense presence of the Catholic Church in the town and the philosophy of self-improvement supported by the labor movement, ethnic and religious differences seemed to play less of a role than the influence of the Church and the mines.

University graduates from Glace Bay in the 1950s and 1960s often moved off the island and stayed away, following their careers, but many returned and established themselves in the town, especially as educators and public officials. One of the reasons class structures in the town are hard to define lies in the success of these university graduates. For families from every neighborhood and economic class, post-secondary education provided the credentials for upward mobility. Traveling to Sydney for a training program or off-island to university in Halifax, Antigonish, Sackville, or Truro, these young people were the pride of Glace Bay. Their education was relatively inexpensive due to the low cost of higher education in Canada at the time.

One woman described her high school days in the mid-1960s. She attended the Catholic high school and later went on to university in Halifax:

> We thought we were the cat's meow. You know what I mean? I remember when we had to get our pictures taken for the yearbook. All the girls wore their sweaters and not everyone had a string of pearls so we would borrow them. When you look at the pictures we're like twins. Every single one with a string of pearls. We were as good as anyone in the world!

Later she described her classmates' pursuit of education:

> Oh yes, they went in droves as soon as the student aid was available. Why not? Almost everyone planned on doing a year or two at Little X, then they'd go on to something else or find a job. The student aid made it possible, but I don't know if they would have gone to university? Like if they hadn't been able to stay at home and go. Me, I had to get out! I went to Halifax as fast as I could!

The large number of Glace Bay students who pursued teaching careers across Canada led one administrator in Ontario to comment, "Glace Bay is the teacher mill of Canada!"

Getting Your Ticket Schooling through the 1970s was an achievement. The town developed and maintained both Catholic and public schools with pride and hope and nurtured their graduates. Students graduating from Glace Bay schools during the decades following the war were relatively successful; jobs and opportunities in the region made the efficacy of schooling real. This began to change, however, as the economy shifted from industry to service and could no longer employ the number of people finishing training programs even if they looked outside of the Cape Breton region for work.

In 1967, the government stepped in to save DOSCO from bankruptcy, beginning what many described as the period of government dependency for Glace Bay and the surrounding region. Aspirations for young people also declined, shifting from a sense of possibility to a burden of necessity. A graduate of St. Michael's High School in 1962 described his younger brothers and sisters who graduated in the late 1960s and early 1970s as being "passive" in contrast to him and his classmates who were ambitious and excited:

> We were on a wave. Our parents were afraid for us because everything was changing, but to us it seemed like there was so much possibility. We didn't have the choice of "The mines or else!" that our fathers had. Maybe because there was nothing here, we felt like anything could happen!

He suggested that the group graduating from high school behind him and his classmates suffered from apathy caused by the recession. "The jobs we were getting when we went out [to Calgary and Toronto] just weren't there when my brothers finished, " he explained.

A nurse working at the public hospital in Glace Bay[7] also remembered the tone of the early 1970s in her neighborhood of Caledonia, the site of the largest layoffs during that period:

> My younger brothers and their friends kept saying, "Let's get out of here before the company kicks us all out." And my mother would cry and try to convince them to stay in school a little longer, but they dropped out and left anyway. They didn't have anything to show for themselves so when the layoffs came in Kingston, they came back again...angry and drinking.

It was during the 1970s that shifts in industrial jobs across North America began to affect the ability of Glace Bay's children to meet their aspirations. For the children and grandchildren of the miners, nurses, teachers, and government officials who made good during the war years and the period of economic growth that followed, the economy no longer offered stable employment without professional education or technical skills. For those with professional degrees, jobs started disappearing as the Canadian government downsized schools, hospitals, and social services. Even for those still interested in going or willing to go into the mines and finish intensive technical training programs, the company stopped accepting new miners into their apprenticeship program in 1981.

The efficacy of schooling began to erode as this generation faced disappointments at home and away. The relative success of earlier generations made it possible to believe in a success ideology fueled by credentials, but as the recession continued and the mines closed, the future of Glace Bay looked grim.

"Our Young Fella": Educational Aspirations

Decisions to stay on the island or to go west were primary for any young person in Cape Breton. In an island economy this is not in itself unusual, but the changing job market in central Canada in the 1980s and 1990s required more than just a willingness to work. One man explained, "Leaving for away doesn't guarantee jobs in today's economy; if you don't have high skills you won't find much anywhere." Young people had to prepare for leaving as much as for competing in the market at home. Staying at home or finding a way to return was a common desire. "Oh, I'd like to go away for a while," one young man told me, "but I'd like to be able to come home in four or five years or so." "We won't be able to stay," another man said, "unless you want to live with your parents the rest of your life."

With improvements in the national economy during the late 1980s, aspirations for young people in Glace Bay were high; most wanted to go to university and acquire professional jobs, but expectations were depressingly low. Parents spoke with frustration about "our young fella" (often gesturing overhead or out the door) and the lack of opportunities. In some cases, "our young fella" was thirty years old or older and still unable to find stable employment. MacLeod (1995) attributes the experiences of family members and the young people themselves as primary influences on how individuals interpret their opportunities. In a town with chronic unemployment, those experiences are likely to be negative, but this situation was not new to Glace Bay and does not accurately explain why aspirations continued to be so high.

Even with recently gained educational credentials, jobs in Cape Breton were hard to find. At the time of my research, the unemployment rate was 25 percent for Glace Bay. Many students stayed in school because of the lack of jobs available to them without a high school degree. Even with that degree, some students found that they "didn't have enough," that their credentials were not competitive and that they had to try for more. One teacher told me with frustration how young people were turning to the government system to survive. He quoted one of his former students who seemed pleased to have gotten enough work to gain unemployment insurance. The student told him, "Oh yeah, sir, I'm doing great! I got my stamps you know, I've got the pogie! I'm doing fine."[8]

I spoke with a young man who graduated from Glace Bay High School in 1994. He admitted that he had not made many proactive choices about his future. As he put it, he was told by his high school counselors to take the careers program, the equivalent of American vocational tracking, and within that program he believed he was not allowed to make many choices about his education. His alternatives since graduating seemed limited because he seemed to have a single-minded focus on getting back into high school to retake his math courses so that he would be more competitive getting a place in a training course or a university program. Glace Bay High School had conducted these post-graduate classes for a number of years but had recently cut back and he was having problems getting in. I asked why he would want to go back to high school after having graduated. "I don't know," he said. "My friends are there, but I don't really want to. I don't know."

I asked if he had any other options and he mentioned his mother wanted him to apply to a computer-training program. He has a computer at home, he said, and he likes to play games on it. I asked if he had spoken to any of the admissions officers, and he said he had to go for an interview or "something." I realized, in this conversation, that the process of actively seeking educational opportunities was frightening for this young man. He knew he had abilities, as he was quick to point out his proficiency at using his computer and the types of books he liked to read, but he also seemed aware of his lack of initiative and was uncomfortable about what to do about it. Unlike previous generations, the ambiguities of the job market both local and outside of Cape Breton made planning for the future uncertain. When I asked about his other interests, however, the young man became very animated. "I like the real-life stories," he said. I asked what kind, and he said he liked mysteries, but real ones with complicated problems. "I like solving puzzles," he said and added, "I'd like to be an investigator for the police or the government." When talking of his dreams, this young man easily described the kind of work he would like and how it matches his perceived skills. His knowledge of how to reach these goals, however, was extremely limited.

The computer course mentioned above could have been one of several offered in the region at the time. MacKenzie College and Compu-college were two of the largest proprietary schools—branch campuses of national organizations. These are shown along with a number of other post-secondary institutions that offer computer training in the table below. Because the young man described above comes from a single-parent, low-income family, he would need financial assistance to go to either of these programs, probably in the form of student loans. His quick response that he could "go get a computer course" was typical for his generation (as was his interest in investigation of "true crime"). Like many schools across North America, Glace Bay teachers and counselors spoke often about the opportunities available across the country for individuals with technological training but rarely specified employers. Over and over in economic development reports, government press releases, and around kitchen tables, the benefits of technological training were heralded as the key to the future.

Table 2: Proprietary and Public Post-secondary Institutions in Cape Breton in 1995

University College of Cape Breton	Mac Tech
Breton Beauty College	Magi Learning Centres
Cape Breton Business College	MacKenzie College
Patrick's Beauty College Ltd.	Commercial Transportation
John Roberts Powers Career School	Training and Consulting
Scruples Hair Care Centre Ltd.	H&R Block Canada, Inc.
Compucollege School of Business	Excel Learning Technologies Ltd.
Nova Scotia Community College	Hairmasters
Sydney Campus	Industrial Cape Breton Youth
Strait Campus	Employment Opportunity
Nautical Institute Campus	New Deal Development Centre
Linkage Research Associates	Centre for Human and
Adult Vocational Training Centre	Organizational Development
Unama'ki Training and Education Centre	

Despite the plethora of training opportunities in industrial Cape Breton, in reality, there were few jobs in the region during the 1990s for those with engineering degrees, much less basic computer skills. This reality was masked in some ways by the popular and very public success of the Cape Breton music industry and accompanying multimedia technology companies. The number of individuals employed in these industries, however, was relatively low and tended to be a product of a grassroots movement in the rural areas rather than industrial Cape Breton County.[9] The assumption that education, especially technological training, could provide an edge—a rare skill that could transform the holder into an economic success—was still widely accepted.

To further explore the aspirations of young people within the town, I conducted an open-ended survey at Glace Bay High School. I met with two large groups of juniors and seniors during their free period in the afternoon.[10] After conducting the survey, the students and I talked about their goals after graduation. As the conversation became livelier, the students warmed up, and one young woman explained her perspective of the future for kids in the town:

> I didn't give you long answers to those questions you asked because I thought you'd be saying bad things about us. It's not a pretty picture here, what with the pogie and the pension checks, but we're not bad people. We all want something from life, all of us. Most of us are going to go to university or get technical degrees. It doesn't matter if you're on assistance or if your mom gets a check. We're just as good as anyone.[11]

Many of the students nodded their heads to these comments, and another student joked about the costs (one of the questions on the survey). "Yeah, you asked if it [education] was worth it," he said. "We'll be paying our loans for the rest of our lives, but what else can we do?"

Many students repeated this sentiment in their survey responses. All of the ninety-seven respondents wrote that they were planning on graduating from high school. All but two of the students stated that they planned on continuing their education after high school. One explained that he would be working with his father in the family business and did not need college, and one said that she did not know but that "college is the only thing to do really, if you want to get a job." In answer to their reasons for their future plans, almost all the students stated that they wanted to get jobs, to be successful, or to make money. In follow-up questions regarding the cost of education and whether or not it was worth it, however, many of the students responded very pessimistically, saying that the costs did not match the return on investment.

The majority of the students responded positively to the question, "What do you think your chances are for reaching your goals?" The reasons they gave, however, demonstrated how aware these young people were of the difficulties they faced and how strong the success ideology was in their interpretation of those difficulties. The students who thought they would reach their goals cited hard work, determination, and faith as their reason for getting there. Those who thought their goals were less attainable cited the lack of jobs and money for education as the primary reasons. These responses reflected a mix of beliefs. They supported an achievement ideology that highlights individual effort while at the same time recognizing the economic forces beyond their control. As a result, although many reported that their parents were unemployed, they viewed that failure ambiguously as a mix of individual deficiencies and systemic economic conditions.

The types of jobs the students described in their plans for the future indicate the continued strength of certain career choices. The table below lists the most commonly cited educational and career plans as indicated in the students' survey responses compared with those described by students graduating from Morrison High School in 1957 in the school annual of that year.[12]

Table 3: High School Aspirations

Glace Bay High School Class of 1995	Morrison High School Class of 1957
social work	social work
teaching	teaching
nursing/medicine	nursing/medicine
secretarial	secretarial/accounting
trade (electrician, plumber, etc.)	engineer/electrician
law, criminal justice	RCMP (police)/law
university	university
business	military

The types of careers aspired to by the students in Glace Bay High School in the 1990s were, obviously, very similar to those aspired to by their parents' generation. Keep in mind that their parents, many of whom graduated from high school in the 1960s and 1970s, experienced much higher success rates in finding employment both locally and off the island with their educational credentials. The similarity in job aspirations between the two generations is understandable in that job opportunities in these occupations, especially those in the social services, remained relatively stable, at least through the 1980s.

Most of the jobs for which Glace Bay residents traditionally trained could be found within its established economic or social service system. The census data presented in the table below includes traditional paths of employment. Many coal miners, for example, displaced by the closing of mines in the 1970s and 1980s, were retrained for other labor-intensive industries like construction and machine operation. Clerical jobs with the coal company became positions in government offices. Processing refers in large part to work at the fish plants. Teaching was one of the strongest professional paths, which may help explain why educational values remained so strong in Glace Bay.

Table 4: Occupational Characteristics for the Town of Glace Bay

Occupation	Male	Female
Management	255	135
Teaching	135	260
Medical Science	120	490
Social Science	260	95
Clerical	235	845
Sales	265	310
Service	405	675
Primary*	450	55
Processing	190	105
Machine	410	30
Construction	650	10
Transport	220	15
Other	310	40
*Includes mining and forestry		

(1991 Census, Statistics Canada)

By the early 1990s in almost all areas of work, a high school diploma, if not post-secondary certification, was necessary. Where a young man might have once gone to work with his father or uncle, he now had to pursue a training course to get the "ticket" necessary for his union card and possible employment. Throughout the history of Glace Bay, certain occupations have been considered "sure things." These were jobs that while perhaps not very glamorous, allowed local residents to stay in the region and still make decent wages. Although many of these jobs required post-secondary credentials and provided middle-class incomes, they were still dependent upon the industrial base. With the decline of that base and the retrenching of government institutions and departments, even paraprofessional jobs were at risk. The competition for jobs that were once considered "sure things" changed the aspirations of young people for their futures, but alternatives to those "sure things" were less clear.

The High School on the Highway
There were a number of tensions involved in providing post-secondary education in a region in which most higher education degrees would be useless without leaving for jobs off-island. Local high school students referred to University College of Cape Breton (UCCB) as "the high school on the highway" because of its location on the road between Glace Bay and Sydney. The label reflected the vocational history of the institution and a perception that the degrees offered there were a compulsory step for finding work. Like high school, university education was seen as a requirement. Attending UCCB, however, was perceived as the bare minimum that a university-bound student could choose to do. There was more than a little elitism in favor of schools off-island, a legacy of previous generations of successful scholars who pursued their education off-island before UCCB was established. Even at UCCB, there was a dichotomy—those students who followed traditional liberal arts paths and those who pursued more vocational training. This was similar, in many ways, to the programmatic divisions that occur at the high-school level.

Born out of an amalgamation of the Nova Scotia Eastern Institute of Technology and St. FX Junior College, UCCB was conceived with a specialized mission:

> ...To assure growth, to meet the "...aspirations of the community for cultural, social and economic reasons," to have a degree program available in the area, and to meet the desire of students to save money by staying at home....The Committee is also particularly aware of the need to serve the overall economic development of the industrial Cape Breton area by an expansion of the college. ("Report to the Board of Governors," September 1970)

The development of post-secondary education in Cape Breton, therefore, unlike the wider scope of older institutions in Halifax and Toronto, was based upon a recognized need for education to improve regional economic conditions. St. FX Extension established its junior college in Sydney in 1951 as a service extension department to provide adult education and the "initial stages of post-secondary education" to financially disadvantaged high school graduates. The provincial government developed the technical college primarily to train industrial and trades workers for the coal and steel industry of eastern Cape Breton. Since community colleges in Canada are the equivalent of American vocational schools, a degree-granting community institution for vocational and academic training was unusual, and, therefore, the founders of UCCB had few examples upon which to draw. By combining the vocational training of the Institute of Technology and the liberal arts and strong social service nature of St. FX Junior College, the advisory committee felt they were addressing vocational, intellectual, and cultural needs in the community.

UCCB has a very peculiar structure as a result of this blending. Departments were set up with an interdisciplinary approach which was intended to "...address the academic discontent that the disciplines of the university do not match life" (Campbell, 1973). This approach attempted to combine the vocational requirements of providing credentials with which a student could pursue employment, while at the same time blending with that training an academic educational experience. This meant that while the institution offered a four-year bachelor's degree, it also offered one-, two-, and three-year programs in various forms of trades training. The "schools" also had unusual mixes of departments— biology and engineering, for example.

UCCB also offered a degree program unique in Canada, a Bachelor of Arts in Community Studies (BACS), which combined liberal arts, field experiences, and career-related coursework. The BACS program, because of its unique nature, did not fit the traditional academic/vocational split. The program evolved from Little X's extension service to meet the social and economic needs of the community. Thus, by feeding into the service system upon which Cape Breton is dependent, the program allowed its students opportunities to stay in the area and use their degrees in ways that were acceptable to themselves and their families. One of the women in the program who had once received social service assistance explained her choice of the BACS degree:

> Being in a position that forced me to go to the government for help, I know what it means to be dependent. I want to be the one who administers those programs. I want to help, to be a friendly face. There's a lot that needs to be done and I understand it because I've been there.

Many of the BACS students made similar comments. For them, a university education was not just a degree but a chance to contribute to their community. Even here, however, with increasing pressures on the employment market, BACS students found it more and more difficult to find or create placements within the region.

The BACS degree provides an example of the shift in the purpose of education in the area from the upward mobility of the individual or the training of the local workforce to a community development strategy. Based on the pedagogical and social theories of Freire and other proponents of process learning, the BACS program was designed to allow the students to "learn how they learn" and prepare themselves for careers in social service jobs. Avoiding a purely vocational approach, the program's students described themselves as learning how to solve problems within their community and to be creative in pursuing job opportunities. Some of the students' projects in the BACS program actually did turn into jobs, not just a co-op placement, but jobs created where there were none.[13]

The BACS program had its detractors, and, from an academic point of view, there were problems regarding how well the students were trained in the methodologies of the social sciences upon which they drew for their field projects. The program, however, did not match traditional disciplinary lines and, in fact, disregarded the boundaries of traditional post-secondary education in order to promote the principles of process learning. Whether or not this offered sustainability was questionable as the funding (but not the need) for community-based job opportunities in social services declined.

The role that UCCB played in the ways that education was defined in Glace Bay was a complex one. On the one hand, the presence of the institution provided an opportunity for local post-secondary education that had been provided only in part in the past. On the other hand, this opportunity, because of the accurate perception that some form of post-secondary training was imperative for finding a job, had started to become a right rather than a privilege. Local residents also disparaged the university as not doing enough in terms of providing solutions for local economic problems. One school board member complained that UCCB should have been providing research to help local leaders make better decisions. UCCB was an undergraduate institution, however, and its faculty were occupied primarily with teaching. The economic development plan for the region also called for UCCB to fulfill its role in engineering and technology support as "one of the key requirements for the support and development of a technology cluster" (Brown, 1994). Again, as an undergraduate institution, UCCB was not in a good position to meet these needs.

Conclusion: Shifting the Burden
Examining the relationship between schooling and aspirations for the future reveals the diversity of ways in which Glace Bay residents have viewed education and success in the region. As Glace Bay's mines closed in the 1980s and 1990s and government offices took on more and more responsibility for social service and economic development, industrial Cape Breton also shifted toward the "new economy." Politicians called for more and more education to meet this change. For "schooling" to be complete in Glace Bay terms, the graduate should have the necessary credentials for a job. Although a grade ten education or less might have sufficed in the 1940s, high school graduation was broadly accepted as being necessary in the 1990s for even the most mundane jobs, and post-secondary education was considered mandatory for stable employment. As a result, many people, young and old, referred to UCCB as the "high school on the highway."

Young people, displaced workers, and adults trying to reenter the workforce understood that post-secondary education was one of the only avenues to employment in Cape Breton. University or college programs with curriculum content based on disciplinary guidelines or administrative prescriptions, however, often did not match the socially perceived needs of these students or the communities from which they came. The potential disconnect between educational content and the value of education is addressed in Pomponio and Lancy's (1986) discussion of the value of education relative to economic stability in New Guinea:

> By focusing on the notion of school as a personal long range investment on the part of parents (and other relatives) who support a student during the school years (both financially and emotionally), the content of the actual material learned in schools becomes irrelevant. In its place are the value assumptions and goal orientations imputed to the educative process, viewed from each perspective (that is village and government school). (p. 44)

For the families in my study, the investment in education and the efficacy it gives the individual were often perceived as more important than the content knowledge gained. Post-secondary credentials were "tickets" to employment in a way that coal company "papers" might have been in the past. What might be learned in a university program was often less important than the potential of the degree earned. Some programs offered training in areas that were completely unfamiliar to local residents and thus were further removed from what students might be able to define as useful knowledge. This could and did lead to tension in the classroom between students who enrolled in classes because they had to and faculty values for intellectual work. Faculty at local institutions bemoaned what they perceived to be the vocational orientation of the students who were "just there for the ticket."

Glace Bay residents once considered the "burden" of education light because knowledge and skills could be gained at relatively little cost. Education was not defined narrowly as certification but often broadly on a continuum from knowledge gained from popular education activities such as reading to skills learned on the job or in a professional training program. As requirements for educational credentials increased formal education became a need, a commodity to be acquired rather than an opportunity to be pursued—or not. As each generation acquired credentials, the town began to stratify in ways distinct from the relationships of the mines that had previously promoted an egalitarian spirit among the workers. The cultural capital of reading, for example, disseminated through the cooperative movement, and the lending libraries had been replaced by the acquisition of credentials. By the end of the century, education was something you had to have in order to distinguish yourself from someone who did not have it and, therefore, be more competitive for jobs.

As discussed in the previous chapter, from its roots as a collection of worker's neighborhoods, Glace Bay evolved into a town with a hierarchical class structure, albeit masked by public rhetoric surrounding the shared history of mining. Class differences were rarely discussed, and conflicts related to social status were avoided if possible. Residents maintained this egalitarian model by telling and retelling "We're all in the same boat" stories of living in a company town. The fact remained, however, that some individuals did better economically and passed on their success to their children through enhanced educational opportunities and raised expectations. As the economic base of the town moved from coal and fishing to a diversified economy, the social structure of the town became more complex and more tied to the market of credentials for employment.

As a by-product of increasing educational achievement in the town, however, some families experienced reduced educational expectations;

when competition increased and the value of low-level credentials decreased, the burden of education did not seem worth the costs (Bedard, 2001). Throughout the town's history, it had always been possible to find work (often lucrative work) without educational credentials. Post-secondary educational aspirations, therefore, were a choice, but not the only means of achieving economic success. With the closing of the mines, however, and the decline of industrial work and skilled labor generally throughout North America, individuals who chose not to continue their education after compulsory schooling became increasingly vulnerable to unemployment and underemployment. How did this group come to define education after compulsory schooling? The next chapter will address how education, or more specifically training, has become a requirement of individuals seeking to find employment and a government strategy for economic development.

Notes

1 MacLeod (1995) contends that the increase in families living for more than one generation in government housing reduces the number of individuals who have personal experience with success.
2 Ironically, both of this politician's children achieved graduate degrees, but neither pursued a liberal arts degree program that their father might have equated with an elite "university" education.
3 Radway's study of the reading of romance novels highlights the plurality of ways readers access popular culture. Her analysis raises the paradox of readers who read popular romances to escape their limiting roles as wives and mothers but in identifying with the plots of those texts reaffirm the desirability of those roles. Similarly, Glace Bay residents may enjoy reading as a way of entering a world larger than that inscribed by the mines and their work but at the same time validate the social hierarchy which causes them to live such hard lives.
4 I was unable to access the archived records of the exact number of students who had pursued higher education from Morrison and St. Michael's that were stored during the move to the new high school.
5 St. Francis Xavier Junior College was established in 1951, and a four-year degree program at UCCB was not established until 1982.
6 St. FX and UCCB representatives often bickered over provincial resources, both claiming that they were responsible for serving Cape Breton's post-secondary needs.
7 The Catholic Hospital, St. Joseph's, was in the process of closing during my fieldwork, and many health care workers were being reassigned or laid off.

8 "Stamps" referred to the number of weeks of employment that earns unemployment benefits. The "pogie" was another name for unemployment insurance similar to being "on the dole."
9 The success of Cape Breton musicians, including the Barra MacNeils, Ashley MacIsaac, and Natalie MacMaster, spawned a small industry boom in "traditional" music and drew attention and resources from the music industry in Los Angeles and Toronto. Young people watched this development with interest, resulting in increased enrollments in "heritage" classes like Gaelic at the university.
10 I surveyed 97 seniors. As a result of scheduling, these students were a mix of both the general (college prep) and careers (vocational) programs. I asked whether I was missing any particular group of students using this method and was told that the only students not in those study hall classes were those out sick that day. Further conversations with parents of low-income students revealed that a number of students would have been suspended or on probation, thus this survey probably did miss some students most at risk of not completing high school.
11 Later she asked to do the survey over: "I thought you were going to say bad things about people on assistance," she said, "and I didn't want to say that my parents didn't finish school."
12 Note that Morrison was just one of the two high schools in Glace Bay in the 1950s. In interviews with residents who graduated from St. Anne's High School during the late 1950s, I asked for their comments regarding this list, and they agreed that the aspirations held by Morrison students were true of their Catholic counterparts at St. Anne's as well.
13 This was the only example I found in my time in Cape Breton of a training program that actually produced jobs that were separate from the educational industry itself or existing job markets.

CHAPTER 4
"Training for What?"

> *In spite of good will and ingenious industrial incentives, we in Cape Breton are not even coming close to creating the required number of new jobs for those who are currently unemployed or underemployed and for those who will be entering the labour market.*
> —*Father Greg MacLeod, 1988*

People in Glace Bay almost always immediately referred to the lack of available jobs when talking about formal education. "Training for what?" I was asked, a question usually accompanied by a cynical smile. "Answer me that. Training for what?" Although government programs had increasingly offered university education to their clients, residents almost always spoke of postsecondary training programs as "school." Since I was known to be studying "school," despite my efforts to broaden this category, I was often asked as "an academic person" in conversations with local residents to devise a plausible answer to the training question, assuming that I would fail or at least underestimate the situation. Most of the people I talked with also called my attention to the fact that training does not in itself create jobs, implying that government rhetoric regarding human capital development, while well meaning, was missing an important economic point. If I gave examples of other individuals finding jobs in Halifax or Toronto, my comments were met with knowing looks. "See," they would say, "the training's no good to us if we want to stay here in Cape Breton." In addition, they accurately pointed out that jobs were getting harder to find off the island as well.

This paradox was one of the reasons I chose the town of Glace Bay and the region of Cape Breton for my research. Like many deindustrializing and declining agricultural regions in North America, Glace Bay residents struggled with questions of how to meet aspirations for success in a rapidly changing economy with very few local opportunities. How did local residents make sense of the positive value of education and the negative reality of unemployment? Why did Glace Bay residents continue to invest their community resources and personal energy in education when the credentials they received no longer provided the opportunities promised or desired? How did government policies toward education as a economic development tool affect how local residents defined education? What happened to human capital investment when that investment was reduced? What other alternatives were there for community development other than an emphasis on individual employment?

Human Capital Development
Following the closing of a series of mines and a downturn in the steel industry, many residents of industrial Cape Breton were forced to turn to the government to help them make the transition to a new economic base. Unemployment was not new to the colliery towns of Cape Breton, but the precarious future of the coal and steel industries compounded by the decline in the Atlantic fisheries prompted the provincial and federal government to play a larger role in providing social support than previously. This took place through the establishment of DEVCO (Cape Breton Development Corporation) in 1969 during a period of confidence in the power of Canadian social welfare programs to respond to "social ills" (McGilly, 1993). After a series of relatively unsuccessful industrial development projects,[1] the provincial and federal governments began introducing training initiatives into Cape Breton's economic development plan. For example, one group of displaced miners went back to school to earn teaching degrees. Another group received training to use their mining expertise in archeological exploration and helped to create the Fortress Louisbourg Natural Historic Site located an hour south of Glace Bay. These programs served relatively few workers, however, and did little to develop alternative kinds of economic stimulus.

As the market demand for credentials across North America increased, government and educational policymakers answered that demand with rhetoric supporting the ideology of success and the need to maintain a competitive edge. The kind of work available in Cape Breton, however, had not significantly changed. Economic development programs in Cape Breton promoted training for technology and entrepreneurial initiatives (individualized, creative, market competition) despite the lack of industries or economic infrastructure to support the graduates of such programs locally. The 1994 strategic planning recommendation for the region states:

> It is necessary to educate our residents as to the new direction of the economy and to provide training that will allow them to take full advantage of the opportunities available. This training should focus especially on science, technology, and entrepreneurial development. (p. 13)

The role of the state in emphasizing the connection between education and economic survival may have overshadowed more affective goals of personal and community development in Cape Breton but certainly capitalized upon the desire of local residents to acquire competitive credentials as described in the last chapter.

Government policies and political speeches of the early 1990s promoted education and training as the salvation for towns like Glace Bay. Unlike many other industrial communities in North America, however, levels of academic achievement in Glace Bay were laudable. Compared with mining communities in Appalachia and Pennsylvania during the same period, Glace Bay had extremely high levels of educational attainment.[2] With the exception of some older workers, almost all residents in the town were literate and had completed at least some secondary education. Many had some form of postcompulsory certification or degree. Again, with the exception of some of the older workers near retirement, miners in the 1990s were not laborers but electricians, engineers, and surveyors with high levels of technical training earned through university or apprenticeship programs. Unlike the early part of the century when miners and their families were considered part of the downtrodden "poor" to be served by programs like the Antigonish Movement, in the era of high-tech industry miners' families are part of the economic middle class.[3] To claim that education was the answer to the economic woes of the region was to ignore these very high levels of educational attainment.

Despite the extent of educational achievement, academic credentials, and vocational training, however, Glace Bay residents continued to be vulnerable to unemployment. Unemployment in 1995 was 26 percent. Most residents recognized that this figure did not include workers who had taken early retirement, given up looking for work, or never worked.

Education for personal survival in Glace Bay required pursuing educational strategies that could provide residents with the most options possible in a difficult employment market. One woman described her strategy of returning to university in order to increase her earning potential:

> I came back for financial reasons. My husband died four years ago and I had four small kids and was on [unemployment] insurance for a while. Then I worked for a small company. They went under and I lost my job. I had no qualifications or anything so I decided to try this. But I like it. I'm glad I did. The kids are confused. They say, "oh Ma, what are you doing?" They think I'm crazy, but they help me a lot.

Another student described the support of his family in returning to school after working in the steel plant, raising his family, and surviving frequent layoffs:

> My feeling is that they [family members] have more confidence in me than I have in myself. I come from a family of nine children and after I passed my first year, right? They said, "We're going to party, boys!" I worked twenty years at the steel plant and I still don't have a steady job. This is the only chance I have really. And hopefully I'll receive something from it. Find a better job. The family reaction was something else. Certain things...like my daughter, she loves the idea of me going to college. I was the only one in my family that got a high school diploma and now I'm the first to go to college. It's a plus for me really.

Public talk about formal education centered on the need to develop specialty skills in order to get jobs. Despite their cynicism, conversations among Glace Bay residents continued to project a hopeful attitude toward continuing education and skills development through training. Postsecondary institutions were consistently talked about in terms of viable economic strategies but often with a twist of self-deprecating humor.

Most of the Glace Bay residents returning to postsecondary programs with whom I spoke viewed school as a positive experience for many reasons in addition to vocational training. While most formal education was considered "school" and residents complained that the training they received would have very little use for them without job opportunities when they finished, they did not talk about education being a waste of time. When I asked an older miner about school, he said, "School was very important to me. Learning was important—it still is!"

The risk that "I'll be too old to get a job" was recognized but rationalized by the positive effects of learning, a sentiment shared and expressed by their families and neighbors. They defined education as a positive experience that increased their self-confidence and self-worth, especially when entering new social contexts of new kinds of employment.

Residents did not, however, define education and training as one in the same. On the one hand, these students described education as self-improvement, including becoming an "educated person" in local terms, and the respect that would entail. Training, on the other hand, like schooling, was a source of information and skills, the value of which was determined by its usefulness. These positive connotations of educational experience reinforced the value of education above and beyond the credentials gained by academic achievement.

I was invited to attend a ring ceremony at the Savoy Theatre—a restored movie house in Glace Bay—by a group of returning students. The event was a public recognition by family and friends of their accomplishments. Each degree candidate walked across the stage to receive a class ring, a ceremony as formal and serious as graduation but focused on the collegiate symbol of the ring rather than the diploma. Community members shared the students' pride—often pointing out friends and relatives who had overcome specific obstacles to "make it" there. Conversations in the foyer before and after the ceremony included joking references to "getting the pogie" and alternative uses (paper airplanes and fire starters) of their diploma. The pursuit of education for the purpose of economic security, therefore, was a multidimensional strategy that included affective and social values for self-improvement as well as economic viability. This is not to understate the very real economic role education played in the lives of Glace Bay residents but to highlight the plurality of ways in which education was perceived.

Training, retraining, and vocational education programs prepared individuals for work in a preexisting structure of production rather than for an unknown future. "Training for what?" the people asked, and therein lies the rub. Local residents were aware of the vulnerability of the regional labor market but rarely were able to suggest alternatives that would be less industry specific and would give them more employment flexibility. Generations of dependence on the coal, steel, and fishing industries and the strong emphasis on technological training in the last four decades led them to continue to insist on the efficacy of schooling and the importance of schooling for a vocation. If you work hard and go to school, they believed, you will succeed. When questioned more closely, however, they were just as aware as economists and government officials of the dangers of putting too much faith in training for dying industries.

"Raising the Price of the Ticket" Ironically, as the trend in government policy shifted from industrial development to human resource development in Cape Breton, policymakers adopted the same rhetoric of schooling for empowerment advocated by the early labor leaders. Seventy years earlier during the strikes, that same government had brought in the RCMP (Royal Canadian Mounted Police) to help the coal company suppress labor activists. In contrast to the labor movement's message of empowerment through education, the government's emphasis on improving educational achievement focused on the development of the individual as an entrepreneur rather than on his or her interdependent role within the community.

The absolute value of education as a condition of social reform introduced by the cooperative movement as a tool for the empowerment of the worker reflected local values of education as more than just economic strategies. Glace Bay residents actively pursued vocational credentials, but there was also evidence of a long tradition of learning for the sake of knowledge as well as specific skills. Glace Bay had a history of community support for its children's dreams, regardless of economic resources, for general university studies and professional credentials even if they could not be used locally. In a national educational system where intellectual learning and vocational learning are seen as distinct categories, the people of Glace Bay struggled to reconcile the two within the practices of individual learners.

Although strategic planning reports emphasized the need for education, especially competitive technological training, and political speeches were full of rhetoric regarding the importance of education, in 1994 the provincial government of Nova Scotia announced a plan to shift funds for general education at the postsecondary level to vocational training. Despite the decrease in educational opportunity this would mean, the shift to occupational education was couched in rhetoric regarding the need to increase the educational achievement of all residents. In effect, while policymakers were downsizing government and cutting funding for education, they were contributing to the perceived need for education. Government press releases stressed that retraining and vocational training programs would still be supported or made more accessible to the unemployed but that university programs would receive less subsidization. These statements implied that egalitarian policies of democratic access to university education were not within the resources of the government.

Counselors at the employment offices described a shift that had already taken place to reduce the amount of time allowed for government-subsidized training. In some cases government programs provided a year or less of assistance for education, thus making the possibility of pursuing upper-level training programs, much less a four-year degree program, difficult. Indeed, in the media coverage of postsecondary policy changes, various politicians made it clear that the budget cuts were intended to decrease public subsidy of university programs in favor of skills training. In a radio interview in the fall of 1994, a politician from Halifax argued for decreasing government funding to higher education. The poor, he said, still aren't going to college despite government subsidies. The lack of enrollment by the poor, however, may have been a product of a combination of policy decisions and employment shifts rather than a lack of response to financial support to institutions or individuals.

Local residents accurately saw faults in the logic of the new government policies, and they responded angrily. The student association at UCCB sponsored a rally with a public forum to address the local politicians. One man stood to speak holding a baby in his arms. "I have to make it," he said, rocking the baby gently. "I have to make it for her as much as for me and if you raise the price of the ticket, it's her you'll be hurting. I can't stay a laborer and give her a future too!" Another woman came to the public microphone and explained her point of view:

> What I'm trying to say, in the most civilized way that I can (because I'm not *educated* yet), is that if you cut education you will create a permanent underclass. I don't want to be on the pogie forever, and education can equal a job. We need to increase the speed of employment. Training is faster, yes, but at the loss of general education. Apprenticeship cannot do what an education can.

The speaker above, unemployed and pursuing an education to increase her chances at getting off unemployment insurance, disagreed with policies leading to a separation of vocational training from a general education. Although many students were pursuing higher education for its vocational value, their goals reached beyond short-term economic gain. Rhetoric regarding education as a development strategy often failed to describe what the public saw as a hierarchy of employment opportunities. A training program, while cheaper for both the student and the government, did not provide the same opportunities for the individual as a general education in a degree program.

Education as Big Business
Government policies in Cape Breton that promoted education as a development strategy concentrated on the entrepreneurial aspects of education that matched political and economic trends toward privatization. As government resources declined, building partnerships with business became increasingly attractive. For example, in the early 1980s, there was a plethora of small business loans distributed in an effort to boost the local economy and reward self-starters. Many of these businesses failed, however, and the focus of the government shifted from providing money to individuals to providing more counseling and training—entrepreneurship training. The point of this training was to develop the individual as a potential industry. At a meeting in Sydney to explain this shift to regional entrepreneurs, small business counselors explained to previous grant recipients that future funds would be provided only for professional development rather than venture capital. The struggling small business owners at the meeting admitted they had a lot to learn but wearily responded that they needed resources to compete with larger businesses (like Wal-Mart) rather than more counseling. While intended to develop grass-roots initiatives, the business of education itself (i.e., self-help seminars, training consultants, etc.) was the primary beneficiary.

One of the most successful educational consulting businesses in the area was the Magi Learning Centre, located in downtown Sydney. The center offered courses for individuals interested in computers or travel agency jobs and also provided training for government employment programs, including the fisheries training program described below. Born, in fact, out of a government development policy to privatize training initiatives, the Magi Centre was an example of the entrepreneurial education businesses of the early 1990s. The owner described his business as market driven. "We sell a product," he explained, educational services which were designed to develop "an exchange of information which will help our clients become more proficient in operating in today's work environment." The way the center was set up, the costs of education to the student were evaluated, not in terms of the value of the credential achieved, but in terms of the return on investment in dollars and cents. The educational entrepreneur gave an example:

> If a forty-five-year-old fisheries worker with grade six education were to go through the linear training program of traditional education, he might be ten years in school before he can realize a return on his educational investment. This is too high a cost for most individuals. Instead, our programs are designed to give individuals the ability to market what they've got, to teach them the philosophy of enterprise and entrepreneurial activity.

While his example was compelling and seemed to acknowledge the value of the experience adult students brought with them to his programs, I asked if his staff of trainers practiced this philosophy of self-promotion. He admitted failure with frustration. He had expected, he said, to contract out the instruction for his training programs. Done this way, he expected that there would be a high turnover of instructors as they found employment in other fields between teaching sessions. The fact that this had not happened, he said, saddened and surprised him. His staff had become part of the business of education rather than exchanging their expertise on the open market.

Education as an economic commodity and a business in the region provided not only the tickets necessary to buy a place in the job market but a place of employment as well. Proprietary educational institutions and public training programs had reinterpreted the ideology of early development efforts like the Antigonish Movement and labor education to empower communities through education as a market-driven enterprise in which individuals positioned themselves in the employment market by "buying" education and "selling" themselves. It is difficult to untangle, in this model of education as a commodity market, where the burden of education falls. Certainly, more educational opportunities were available, but for what purpose?

The "Pogie": Education as Unemployment Insurance

With 26 percent unemployment, government social service programs were desperate to provide some source of income to vulnerable Glace Bay families. "Grants" programs, popular in the 1960s and 1970s, whereby the unemployed were given work to keep them afloat until the economy picked up, were obviously difficult to sustain in regions where the economy was fundamentally changing. Retraining was needed, but the norms and practices of existing social assistance and grants programs were well entrenched. As a result, new training programs were often seen as a new form of social assistance, education as unemployment insurance.

The government was a major source of funding for postsecondary schooling, including university education, either through student bursaries or special programs, which were, in turn, heavily influenced by policies of economic development rather than philosophical enlightenment. Although couched in terms of social welfare and reform, the relationship between the government and training was heavily influenced by the need to maintain social harmony by reducing the number of unemployed. In many ways, government support of education for the unemployed had become a new form of unemployment insurance, a stopgap between employment and social assistance.

For residents of Glace Bay during the mid-1990s, the regional government unemployment offices that supported educational strategies included the federal Canadian Resources Development Centre and the Community Employment Resource Office, run jointly by municipal and provincial governments. These offices contracted or purchased a certain number of seats or placements in regional postsecondary institutions and contracted training for special programs like The Atlantic Groundfish Strategy (TAGS) described further below. Although government objectives for training might have included increasing the ability of individuals to find work, they did not specify how that training benefited the individual learner. The goals of the students receiving government training grants were complex in that going to school was associated with getting assistance, getting a job, and cultural values of self-improvement.

Paying for education also complicated the question of the purpose of training. Although some institutions offered special programs designed for government assistance recipients, employment offices referred many of the unemployed to special 80/20 contracts in regularly scheduled courses. This meant that the government paid 80 percent of the tuition and the student 20 percent. The parameters of training grant policies and those of these institutions were not likely to match routinely. Training grants rarely paid for books or the equipment necessary for some vocational programs and there were often problems in coordinating class schedules with students' work schedules (even programs with evening classes). Course dates also had to be coordinated with unemployment checks and/or training grants, often leaving recipients without income for periods of time, which sometimes caused them to drop out of a program to scrounge up more money.

The following were some of the possible ways of receiving government assistance for postsecondary education at the time of my research:

- If you were currently on UI (Unemployment Insurance), then your tuition for training programs would be paid by the HRD (Human Resources Development), which some people referred to by its old name, the CEIC (Canada Employment and Immigration Center), and most just called Manpower.
- If you were on social assistance, then your tuition would be paid by the CERC (Community Employment Resource Center), but there was a limited amount of money available.
- If you were not a client with either program, you would be eligible for Student Aid (government-supported student loans). Student Aid was only applicable, however, to trades or skills training and would not pay for academic upgrading such as literacy tutoring or basic math.
- No matter which approach you took, government-funded "seats" were limited, and you might have had to wait a year or more before you could begin your training unless, of course, you could pay for it yourself.

Add to this list the complicating factors of diverse educational backgrounds and learning styles of clients, and the task of providing quality postsecondary education through a government bursary system seems overwhelming. Obviously, the process of upgrading the academic credentials of the unemployed, a necessary step to be eligible for employment in the very competitive Cape Breton job market, was more difficult than as described in political rhetoric.

When I asked one of the community services counselors whether she felt the system worked, she said she thought they do a lot of good, but that they could do more. The problems of acquiring educational credentials for those lacking basic skills were particularly acute. This group of clients tended to be older and out of school for many years. For students with low levels of literacy, there was not much any of the training programs could do since the clients could not be put into computer upgrading curriculums, and they could not be enrolled in trades training programs without getting an upgrading certificate, regardless of their work experience. Adult education and basic skills training were available in evening classes at the high school and at the adult vocational center, but these programs took time. Individuals with basic skills diplomas were not as competitive for "seats" in upper-level training or university programs, and student loans were not available for basic skills education so this group had to wait for government assistance or pay their own tuition.

Many of the adult learners who received government assistance went through the Adult Vocational Training Center (AVTC). This process resulted in receiving certificates that could then be used to gain entry into other training programs. The process was lengthy with many steps and stages. The AVTC also competed with private training institutions such as Compucollege or MacKenzie College. These private training institutions also received government funds, but the AVTC was significantly cheaper.

The Cape Breton Community College (CBCC)[4] offered vocational training and some service training. Space was limited in most programs; each year they accepted the top students, and the rest were placed on a waiting list until the course was closed. Students who were not accepted had to go through the process again the next year. Competition for space in community college vocational programs was tough. Similar to technical colleges in the United States, the CBCC was the next step for adults receiving basic skills upgrading and for high school students interested in trades. Thus, students who graduated with low scores from high school or older workers with recently acquired basic skills certificates were not as competitive in the admissions race as other applicants were with good high school grades.

So where did that leave the aspiring adult learner? Competition for enrollment, bureaucratic student financial aid, and slippage between training schedules and other social service programs privileged those students who were able to transfer directly from high school into post-secondary training with solid academic records. Government assistance for education often resulted in dead ends because of the competition for placement in upper-level training programs. I often ran into unemployed workers who were "waiting on a course" or had been "put on the list," although they were often unclear about what kind of education they would be receiving or how it would help them in the job market. Almost everyone it seemed was at some point of contact with educational training, but the processes of enrollment were talked about more than what was actually being learned.

In an interview with one of the community service administrators in Glace Bay, I was told that the whole training strategy had "gotten too big for them and it's escalating." He explained that training just for the sake of keeping the unemployed busy or to give them skills for jobs that do not exist had become a policy without purpose:

> That's right. They're training for something that's not there. Training just for the sake of training. I don't understand why they [the unemployed] basically haven't revolted. There is an incredible hostility and lack of faith in their programs by the man on the street. Last week they announced a twenty-week [works] grant out at the college which would be administered at ten o'clock Monday morning. Seven hundred people were there by ten o'clock Sunday night. That makes the loudest statement I can think of. Don't tell me these people don't want to work! We have to change our way of doing business.... We need to be able to invest in education not spend on training....These training programs are jobs to these people.

He pointed out that local officials recognized the difference between training and education as well as the students participating in the programs. Desperate for an answer to consistent unemployment, he explained that counselors saw providing new knowledge sets of any kind as a better solution than just paying out unemployment and eventually social assistance.

The administrator went on to say that things had improved in Glace Bay since the late 1980s, but that he was seeing more and more families receiving welfare with low morale and little incentive to go to work or school. In my interviews with social assistance clients, in one case a third-generation recipient, his comments were confirmed, if perhaps in less pessimistic terms. In many cases, my informants were not discouraged about education as an abstract concept or as a general value; in fact, most still insisted on the efficacy of schooling. They did point out that perhaps the employment opportunities available were not worth the cost of the training programs.

I asked about grant syndrome and grant addiction, common criticisms by people both within the town and outside observers, and the administrator said that in his experience, the men get tired of grant work and will eventually try for something better. This observation is important. There was a great deal of negative commentary in the press, especially in central and western Canada, regarding the dependency of

Maritime regions on government handouts. Local residents, including the counselor with whom I spoke, were not unaware of these perceptions. How they interpreted the use (or abuse) of government programs, however, included locally based assumptions about government, work, and individuals' rights.

As an educator, I wondered about the "lumping" of educational programs into the same category as green projects (a type of grant work which includes beautification jobs such as constructing a new walking path alongside the brook leading into the harbor and seasonal work such as shoveling snow from sidewalks). I asked if participants were sometimes put into training programs when work was not available to them just for the sake of keeping them busy. The unemployment counselor agreed but pointed out that training would be beneficial regardless. Did this imply that just by being in an educational facility, the individual would learn? I asked critically. He said yes, but that there would always be some for whom there wouldn't be any learning and they wouldn't pick things up by osmosis.

Government assistance for education in Cape Breton, therefore, was a complicated system of egalitarian policies of social assistance and strategies for maintaining a viable workforce. Many of the unemployed saw these mandates as required schooling for assistance. In other words, school was becoming work in itself—a means to a paycheck rather than a means to a job. Credentialing, in the sense of getting a chance or qualifying for a more attractive employment option, was becoming secondary to the government's need to provide the unemployed with a proactive way to earn government support and to become self-sufficient. Notions of personal efficacy and empowerment were implied, but the reality of the low-level vocational nature of the educational opportunities available reflected a continuance of the separation between vocational and general education for the purposes of "development" and meeting government objectives. Although increased schooling for the purpose of better employment was an objective accepted and applauded by local residents, individual aspirations for self-improvement were often more involved and training for the purpose of providing "something for the unemployed to do" certainly did not meet these complex goals.

The following case study provides an example of a particular government grant program, The Atlantic Groundfish Strategy (TAGS) serving the fishing community of Glace Bay and the region. The fishing community included both small businesses and a labor pool of fishermen and processing workers. Although the fishing industry in Glace Bay was historically smaller than that of coal or steel, it was undergoing similar transitions in the late 1980s and early 1990s as those experienced by miners in the 1960s because of the closing of the Atlantic fisheries. Workers and fishermen in this industry had different experiences than those of the miners, but their struggle with the closing and the decline of the industry overall offers an opportunity to examine how local residents reconciled educational values toward training and education with economic development.

The TAGS Program: A Case Study
During an interview with a human resources counselor about the rise in dependence on government transfer payments in Glace Bay, I asked how participants perceived labor transition training programs intended to alleviate unemployment. My informant, an unemployment counselor and a Glace Bay native, explained cynically that government assistance for education might only serve to keep the unemployed off the UI (unemployment insurance) for a period of time, not solve the problem. Many of the unemployed, he explained, were in denial. They saw grant work and training allowances as temporary measures to hold them over until they return to the kind of work that they did before. "The fishing community is especially resistant to change," he said. "At first they stayed home and stewed," he continued, referring to the time in the early 1990s when the fishing grounds began to be restricted. Five years later, however, they were starting to work in the grant programs and training programs, and there was a marked difference in their attitudes.

Participants in the Atlantic fishing industry have had a long-term relationship with the government, as it was the government that made regulations regarding licensing, net size, etc., as well as eventually making the decision to close the fisheries. At a press conference announcing an agreement between the federal and provincial governments to assist "individuals and communities affected by the decline in the ground fisheries" (The Atlantic Groundfish Strategy or TAGS), I listened to government officials and educational administrators talk about the role of education in economic recovery. Although coal mining and the related steel industry are historically the largest industries in Cape Breton, the closing of the Atlantic cod fishery because of a depletion of stock affected the entire Maritime region.

Some of the officials at the TAGS press conference talked about the changes in the types of available jobs in a service economy and the need for retraining to meet those job requirements. One solution mentioned was to create a partnership between school, education, and work. "Somehow they got separated, but we're trying to put these things together," a politician said. Other rhetoric included the need to give people a "new view" to spread the "vision," implying that social reform was necessary to convince the workers of the efficacy of schooling.

Glace Bay residents of all educational levels and occupations including fishing had clearly expressed to me their belief in the efficacy of schooling. Rhetoric surrounding economic development strategies, however, continued to highlight the need to "instill" such a belief in the under- or unemployed. This case was no different. The emphasis on social reform for fisheries workers may have been a commentary on the differences between fishing, which does not in itself require academic credentialing, and other occupations within the region. Fishing was an honorable tradition in many Glace Bay families and the knowledge necessary for success was passed on through apprenticeship from one generation to the next not through formal educational programs. Working at the fish plant, on the other hand, was considered honest work but not a career to pass on to your children.

TAGS, designed to assist the fisheries workers and fishermen, required beneficiaries to go through counseling, whereby they would establish an "action plan" for themselves, usually including some form of schooling, before receiving their benefit package. Policymakers described the new assistance program as a way to give the fisheries workers "hope, a chance to move into other careers and active personal improvement" and to develop a "culture of lifelong learning." In this regard, I had found no evidence that the residents of Glace Bay in any occupational group, including fishing, were culturally deficient with regard to values for education as self-improvement; in fact, the opposite was true. Language of vision, personal improvement, and lifelong learning was pervasive and promoted in all levels of public talk regarding education in the town. The value of knowledge was evident in all aspects of everyday life as well as in the workplace.

For example, Claire, one of my neighbors, worked in the fish-packing plant down by the harbor. Coming by after work, she would often drop in to deliver some fresh mackerel fillets, her clothes dirty and smelling of fish. Claire knew about my research and often started conversations with me about things she had read. She liked history and reading about faraway places and described herself as someone who liked to learn. Usually our conversations focused on travel, historical events, and union issues at her plant but rarely on formal education. A high school graduate, Claire subscribed to a historical magazine and enjoyed talking about the things she had read. On one of these visits, she asked me if I wanted to go with her to the unemployment office to go see a counselor about the new assistance program (TAGS). We went to the government office building at Senator's Corner, and I waited while Claire met with her counselor.

At the meeting, the counselor told Claire she did not need to come in to the office since she was still working. They discussed how long the fish plant would stay open, and the counselor suggested to Claire that she start thinking about what she wanted to do if it closed. She told her that she would be eligible for all five years of the TAGS program at the minimum of $211 a week and that she would be eligible for work on green projects. As an afterthought, she mentioned that Claire might want to think about training. On the way home, Claire said she would think about training, but she was probably too old for university. Although Claire spoke often of her ideas and questions she had about the world derived from her reading and vacation travel, the active pursuit of higher education did not seem to be an option for her. When I asked what area of training she thought she might pursue instead of university, she replied that she didn't know. "I was good in school," she said brightly, but then fell uncharacteristically silent for the rest of the ride home.

In my conversations with Claire, I learned that reactions to the closing of the fisheries differed depending on where you worked in the industry. For the workers in the fish plants, it meant the end of their jobs but not necessarily of their careers. As unskilled labor, many of them were not committed to the fishing industry, merely to the paycheck that the plant offered. The closing of the Atlantic fishery was upsetting to them because it meant the closing of one of the few industries left in the region for unskilled labor, especially for women. This was a harsh blow for workers who had few other skills to offer. The fishermen, however, often had their life invested in their boats as well as generations of family history. Their skills, although limited to fishing, were often more sophisticated than those of plant workers due to the multitask nature of fishing, and they interpreted the closing of the fisheries on a more personal level than one of pure economics.

To find out more about the TAGS program and how the individuals who participate were informed about its offerings, I attended an information session held at the Army/Navy Hall behind the Post Office. The hall was a social club with an atmosphere of a community-gathering place, and you could see the dartboards and the little counter that served as a bar, although the room had been set up for the meeting. The room itself was small and close. As I walked in, there were three women in business suits sitting at a table facing a group of women from the fish plant, who sat in the first few rows of seats to one side of the room. Claire sat among them. The back rows of chairs were filled with men, old and young, dressed in overalls, work pants or jeans, sweat suits, jackets, and baseball caps. I walked to the far side of the room, across from Claire, and sat behind a small group of men who looked like reporters or perhaps interested townspeople. Although I did not want to align myself with "the authorities," no one on my side of the room looked like they represented the politicians or bureaucrats in their suits, and I hoped I would be perceived as neutral, if that were possible.

The presentation started with introductions by a representative from the Fisheries Industry (the labor union). She introduced herself, emphasizing her position with the union, and then introduced the panelists—counselors and information officers from Human Resources and Social Services. She explained that the meeting that night was intended to be a general information session and that questions would be taken, but answers might not be available, since the program was so new. She explained what we all knew, that TAGS stood for The Atlantic Groundfish Strategy and was designed to help with the restructuring of the fishing industry in Atlantic Canada. She then went over a list on a large presentation pad propped on an easel at the front of the room. The TAGS program was supposed to facilitate labor market adjustment of participants, enhance the profession of fishing through improving skills of people remaining in the industry, and facilitate community economic rebuilding. The representative stressed to the group that the program was not to remove people from the industry altogether but to restructure it by helping people retrain for other "areas," helping those who stay in, and helping the communities affected by the crisis in the industry.

In the course of her explanation of the basics of eligibility for the program, a man at the back of the room interrupted. He stood and aggressively made a comment about the way the program takes people out of the fishing industry and puts them into substandard training programs for occupations that do not match the skill level and income level of fishing. The union representative did not respond but nodded and made conciliatory gestures. Throughout her presentation, she occasionally made comments that reminded the crowd that she worked for the industry rather than the government. For example, in response to a comment by a man who complained he'd recently been trying to feed four people on $4.50 a meal, the representative responded that she and her family had lived on Kraft dinners, too, and that they would all do what they could. The crowd, however, continued to challenge her and did not seem to buy into her assertions that "we're all in this together," despite her union credentials.

Both the panelists and the group of observers at the front of the room seemed to disregard the comment regarding substandard training, skill levels, and income. From what I had learned about the fishermen who maintain viable businesses in town, however, the speaker had an important point. A lobsterman, a few people told me, could make over $60,000 a year in the few months of the season and then collect unemployment the rest of the year. (I was never able to confirm this example, although fishermen and townspeople alike commonly accepted it as true.) Likewise, if you owned your own boat, you could make a fair profit each year, although the closing of the fisheries no longer made that income from ground fish possible. To introduce such businessmen to a training program for an entry-level position in the construction industry was indeed overlooking their previous skill levels and income, not to mention the autonomy they had experienced as self-employed business owners. This difference between the fishermen and the plant workers in the room was an unspoken component of the meeting.

The fisheries representative then went on to describe how an individual would continue to remain eligible while on the program. She explained how in the past you could "sit back and do nothing but collect your check" and how the people in northern Canada were "angry about supporting people for nothing." Flipping a page of her chart, she pointed to a list of program requirements. In the TAGS program, she said, you were required to be "active" 80 percent of the time. This meant either actively looking for work, training for work, or working. According to the strategy, each person would receive extensive counseling and would devise an "action plan." She explained, "For example, if you still intended to fish, your plan might be to fish from May to November and then enroll in a training program from December to April." I looked over at Claire and she was shaking her head. Later she explained her reaction, saying that if her five minutes with the unemployment counselor had been "extensive counseling," then they were all in trouble.

The man in the back stood up again and said that in the old program (TAGS was not the first government assistance program for the fisheries) the people "had to go to school." Another man stood and told a story about his friend who had been forced to take a heavy-equipment training course even though he was uncomfortable with the job. An argument followed as one of the other officials at the main table, a representative from the unemployment office, responded defensively. "He wasn't forced," she maintained. "Didn't you tell him to 'try it again'?" the man answered. He went on to explain that his friend "felt" he had to do the program, because he could not get his concerns across to the counselor. Another man at the back of the room said he was not forced to go to training, but he was told to go in order to participate in the program and thought training was required to receive his benefits.

As the meeting progressed, another question came from the back of the room about the differences in renumeration for green projects workers and those in training. Questions also arose about how you could go back to work if you were involved in a training program. Most of the questions addressed the differences in perceived and real compensation for participating in a training program compared with that received for working on a short-term grant project. The fisheries representative continued to try to respond to the questions and methodically move on to the next point on her flip chart.

After saying nothing for the first part of the meeting, a woman sitting with the fish-plant workers spoke up and asked belligerently, "Who makes the rules?" and the union representative, clearly tired, responded bluntly, "Ottawa!" Another man asked why his pay was different from another's. She explained that each person's pay would be different because of the different histories of unemployment compensation and that different pay scales would be applied for different lengths of "active" time. Another man responded that the government might want him to work a certain number of hours, but that his training program required the same work from every man—a certain length of time on a machine, for example. He gave an example from his experience with the heavy-equipment training program. He also made the point that because of the requirements of his training program, he was making less than minimum wage. He sounded tired and frustrated as he explained his position to the panel at front of the room:

> I'm not saying I didn't want the training," the man said, "I'm just trying to make sure that these people understand what's happening. You're telling these people one thing, but you're not telling them that it's not black and white. There are lots of gray areas out there, and lots of ways that people can fall through the cracks.

At this point the crowd stopped listening to the presentation completely, and conversations arose around the room as the fisheries representative continued to read off her flip chart.

Then another question about training came up, and the crowd became more attentive. "If you get training for another occupation, can you still be a fisherman? Will the government let you go back to fishing? Will they give you back your license?" Eileen started to answer, then stopped, and then said, "No." The question hung in the air and for once the room was very quiet. Granted, for those who worked in the fish plant, not returning to fisheries work was probably not perceived as a fatal blow. For many of the fishermen, however, the sea was their life's work and for many families, a legacy of generations. Everyone in the room was aware of the enormity of this loss, but, again, the diversity of the population served by the TAGS program became clear. Not all the participants had the same interest invested in fishing, nor did they have the same aspirations toward training for other careers.

The fisheries union representative closed up the meeting by saying that they would take names and numbers and get back to the people with questions that they had not been able to answer. During the meeting, about three people had gotten up and left, either saying nothing or muttering about it being bullshit. At one point, a man came in from outside and shouted at Eileen that she didn't know what she was talking about. The man sitting next to me, who turned out to be a retired miner who sometimes rents equipment to his fishing neighbors, said the irate man was a regular at meetings like this and you got used to him interrupting. In some ways I had expected more people to react more vocally, but the quiet murmuring of the people, even though many were complaining, seemed to indicate what the employment counselor had said earlier was true. They were starting to realize that their lives as fishermen were never going to be the same.

Conclusion

Education as an economic development strategy for individuals displaced by deindustrialization has many challenges—dissonance between skill levels developed in training and those previously held, gray areas between educational curriculum and real-life schedules, low return on investment in training due to a lack of jobs, and dependence on a complicated bureaucracy of government funding to gain access to training programs. Unfortunately, many of the unemployed or displaced in Cape Breton did not seem to know what they needed even when the government tried to ask for their feedback.

Education as a social welfare strategy offers complex challenges. Riemer (1997) emphasizes the seemingly no-win situation for individuals who try to leave social assistance through training programs that provide low-skills training. In most cases, she explains, the jobs that are available after completing training are undesirable in some way—requiring too much physical labor, lacking excitement or worker autonomy, or having no potential for advancement. Even for the most ambitious of the trainees, the reality of the job market for which they are trained is a daunting and eventually demoralizing experience. Riemer offers interesting alternatives:

> Assuming instead that moving onto the job ladder requires not just a first step, but second and third steps as well....Competency based models, with broad-based funding and multiple-target groups, can also offer training in skill areas that include high and low technologies, and can accommodate choices based on interests and skills rather than categorical group membership and academically sanctioned knowledge. (1997, p. 107)

To provide training to the unemployed, therefore, requires looking past their initial training program to their successful placement in jobs that they feel are appropriate for their lives. It means accommodating individual choices and cultural values as well as considering development strategies for the larger region. In an area that already has more than enough competent plumbers and electricians, to insist that trades training or service industry training is a developmental solution is to ignore the deficit of viable employment opportunities. Is employment, however, the only indicator of success?

In some ways the problem in Cape Breton went beyond the lack of jobs or the lack of resources to retool one's skills to a psychological dependency upon the expertise of outsiders. In an interview with an older man who had gotten into the insurance industry after leaving the mines in his late twenties, I asked what problems he saw in job training in the 1990s, compared with when he apprenticed for the coal mines in the 1950s. "Training for what?" he asked, not surprisingly. When he apprenticed, he told me, there were jobs available. He worked in the mines as well as the steel plant. He was even able to get out of the mines and into business when he wanted to. Now there's no chance of industry jobs, he said, only service ones and they don't provide security. "It's a pipe dream," he sighed.

He saw no way for his children to raise their families in Glace Bay. Although his daughter had a teaching degree and his son had a position with the government, he did not believe the kind of growth that would support his family into the next generation was possible in Glace Bay. "There isn't anything for the next generation," he said, "they either blew it or it never existed." The lack of jobs and government "handouts," he argued, have destroyed what little initiative there is left. He gave an example:

> When we get job applicants, they have two attitudes: either they have a university degree and they say I'll take anything regardless of pay just to have a job, or they have no degree and their first question is "What's the pay?" If it's not enough, they don't come back.

For many of the unemployed, low-paying jobs may not have offered as much to them as the pogie or government grant work. At least with government work or grants you had opportunities for education or funds to relocate off-island.

The unemployed were a particularly important group in Glace Bay for understanding how education acts as a site of cultural contest and contradiction. The unemployed included members of every family in the town, in all income brackets, occupational groups, and neighborhoods. While many were "educated" in the sense of academic credentials, their education was useless unless they could adapt to the "innovative" nature of a knowledge economy (Drucker, 1993). Given the opportunity, the application of residents' local literacy might have been more effective in negotiating the regional economy than a university degree or training certificate. It was certainly useful in the entrepreneurial networking of the informal economy (although sometimes outside the law). The formal system of post-compulsory education, however, did not provide space for such experiments, and most training programs in the area did not emphasize the development of knowledge-producing skills.

In an important way, Glace Bay's unemployed population included those individuals without jobs who were living "away" in Ontario, Alberta, or British Columbia. Shuttle migration or the moving back and forth from one region to another meant that workers often left their Cape Breton "home" to find work and returned home when that work became unattractive or unavailable. When family members returned to Glace Bay because of unemployment despite their training or educational achievements, the efficacy of education was further eroded. Conversely, the "Bay Boy" identity of those living away in central Ontario was called into question by deteriorating economic conditions at home. As a coal-mining town, the image of the "simple life" in Glace Bay, while economically vulnerable, was also somehow heroic and righteous. Workers living away could call upon the legacy of coal, close-knit communities, and scrappy survival to establish their own identity in the working-class neighborhoods of Ontario and Alberta. As unemployment and government dependency increased at home, however, the image of the scrappy survivors faded. Even while instructing me on the wonders of their Cape Breton home, Glace Bay emigrants would make disparaging comments about the amount of government support and the ways that people in Cape Breton were getting "something for nothing" while those in Ontario struggled.

Practices of "leveling" which traditionally served local residents well in maintaining a local identity in opposition to an external authority were less viable, in some ways, in a knowledge economy. Regardless of the economic development of industries in the region, if training programs continued to focus upon base-level vocational skills rather than empowered forms of education (which does not in itself exclude vocational programming), then those without education would continue to do worse than their counterparts in town.

I do not have an answer for my Cape Breton friends who asked, "Training for what?" Education seemed, however, to be actively and optimistically pursued in the town despite this lack of answers. The efficacy of schooling in Glace Bay was closely related to the high value placed upon children and their futures in the town. Despite the negative forecast by some, this was, after all, a town of survivors, and giving up did not seem to be an option. The paradox of investment in education for which there is no return was also a clash between local residents' broad hopes and expectations for themselves and their children and the narrow views of development strategies that focus on economic development without consideration of social values for success. Definitions of success in Glace Bay also included the desire to have a choice of whether to stay in Glace Bay or move away and not to be forced to leave. What was good about Glace Bay, what was local and cherished, may not have been recognized in economic development planning.

Notes

1 These projects included a heavy-water plant located between Glace Bay and the town of Donkin to the south and an industrial park north of the city of Sydney.
2 Only 50 percent of the residents over twenty-five of Cumberland City, Kentucky, for example, a town with a very similar economic history to Glace Bay, held high school diplomas as of the 1990 census. Similar rates of attainment are true for mining regions in western Kentucky, Ohio, West Virginia, and Pennsylvania.
3 The average income for a miner in 1994 was $40,000 (Canadian).
4 The AVTC was amalgamated into the community college system in the late 1990s.

CHAPTER 5
Local Literacy

"Who's your father?"
—Local saying

In the course of collecting individuals' "learning histories," I asked residents to describe what sources of information they felt were important. Who did they go to when they needed to make important decisions? How did they gain the knowledge necessary to negotiate everyday kinds of challenges? They unanimously responded that their decisions were informed by dialogue with trusted friends, from reading, watching TV, and listening to the radio. School or training was rarely mentioned, even from those with advanced degrees. When it came to an "everyday" literacy, they talked about multiple sources of information. In narrating stories to me about wisdom, the people I interviewed stressed the interplay between local networks and individual self-improvement. Although the teller may have completed or been participating in postcompulsory education, the knowledge acquired in formal schooling was referred to as personal rather than communal. Fluency in shared knowledge, although informed by individual learning experiences, was what was used to determine local wisdom.

My discussion in the last two chapters addressed changes in the efficacy of education in Glace Bay and the role of education in economic and community development. With the extreme downsizing of coal and steel industries, economic development initiatives and requirements for educational credentials focused more and more on the individual learner as entrepreneur. How did this make use of or affect local systems of knowledge acquisition and production? Why did local residents seem reluctant to participate in entrepreneurial schemes separate from traditional modes of economic production and ways of knowing?

In *Local Knowledge*, Clifford Geertz (1983) explains that common sense is a cultural system, a system that can be examined by investigating the convergence between experiential knowledge and colloquial wisdom. Glace Bay residents spoke often of the value of both. Glace Bay residents relied on a "folk" knowledge of home more than a realistic appraisal of the Maritime economy to construct their local identity. Understanding the construction of a traditional "folk" identity, whether a product of recent movements toward tourism or a defensive response to economic vulnerability, helps untangle the puzzle of why a community that was moving forward toward an educated knowledge- and service-based economy would stick so stubbornly to an experiential and colloquial form of knowledge as its primary basis for building identity. Individual economic success in Glace Bay at the end of an industrial era, regardless of educational credentials, was tied to historically constructed local frameworks of knowledge.

This is not to say that academic learning was separate from local knowledge. Self-education through reading, participating in public dialogue, and pursuing a formal education were all learning activities which echoed the town's historical legacy of education as a liberating practice which prioritized the empowerment of knowledge. In listening to individuals' stories regarding their education, formal and informal, I found that while local residents believed formal education and training programs could earn you the ticket necessary to apply for the job, it was the ability to share and exchange information that was valued and respected as a resource for making everyday decisions and actually finding employment. The exchange of information was not just a survival strategy; residents of the town enjoyed a lively conversation. This sharing of stories, facts, figures, and assorted trivia is reminiscent of oral cultures and reinforces the value of traditional practices as security against an unpredictable world (Giddens, 1994). Learning, therefore, whether in school, a community class, or in a newspaper or book, provided a kind of local literacy that informed the everyday practices of the community. The primacy of learning helped realize in some small ways the ideal of education for empowerment as well as skills training or gaining credentials.

External sources of information—television, radio, books, and print media as well as correspondence courses and church study groups—provided information that added to local conversations and to individuals' personal explorations. When I was sitting in coffee shops around town, residents would often comment on how hard I was working "at my papers." Occasionally someone would ask me what I was studying, and I would tell him or her about my project in Glace Bay. Oh yes, they would say, education is terribly important. I tried, when appropriate, to turn these encounters into interview exchanges and ask the person about their education. One woman summed up many of the responses I received:

> Oh, it's not what you learn, it's just the learning. If you keep learning you'll never stop growing. Facts and figures don't really mean all that much, though they help you settle an argument if you're good. I'm good at that in my family, they ask me when they don't know.

The primacy of learning as an important cultural value was evident in this comment and played an important part in framing how local residents pursued opportunities to access and acquire information.

Rather than marginalizing information learned in academic contexts, individuals incorporated school knowledge into local knowledge where possible. Operating on a continuum, learning was respected for its intrinsic value rather than curricular content. When I tried to separate academic learning from local knowledge by asking about "school" learning versus "community" wisdom or smarts, my informants would protest the dichotomy between the two, citing that the learners themselves were not considered to be restricted from either environment. What was considered "useful" in local dialogues, however, might have contributed to a devaluing of what was learned in school if it had no practical application in everyday activities. In looking at education from the learner's perspective, the practice of education as knowledge acquisition and transmission became a strategy that crossed classifications.

If learned skills were not useful in the region, vocational education or training would lose value. For example, if an individual completed a course in heavy machine operation but could not find work on a job site, the usefulness of that training might be questioned. In this case, an academic course in communications or organizational theory might have been more useful for negotiating complex social networks or political bureaucracies. The usefulness of knowledge, therefore, crosses distinctions of vocational or general, formal and informal in the practices of the individual learner.

Narrative and discourse, in particular, were key forms of knowledge and sense-making in Cape Breton. In addition to the creation myths and booster tales used by Glace Bay residents to describe their town and build a sense of community identity, the discursive position of the individual within the town also had real importance in negotiating what I call local literacies. Similar to Illich's notion of vernacular activities, local literacies are ways of knowing that lead to productive practices that allow community survival and success. Personal narratives described multiple ways of interacting within the town and without and yet also indicated the ambiguities held by residents trying to negotiate an uncertain future. Although narrative conventions help create community identity by blurring distinctions and rationalizing conflict, they also provide a discursive space in which individuals can cross boundaries and act within various social contexts.

My point in writing this chapter is to show that these literacies (academic, local, and personal) were not separate in the sense that all actors can play multiple roles and use the information they acquire in a variety of settings. A change in those settings, however, results in ambiguities as to the usefulness of certain forms of knowledge. These ambiguities often result in uncertainty and a lack of confidence in the future. In the following sections, I discuss local examples of networking, the processes of knowledge acquisition through self-education and discovery, and the ways in which residents used multiple literacies to negotiate success for themselves and their community.

Everyday Literacy
Practical knowledge, the everyday trading of information about family, work, household economies, and sports, was highlighted in Glace Bay conversations in many ways. This kind of knowledge, whether conveyed as gossip, conversation, explanation, or taught through hands-on lessons, was part of the cultural capital of the town.[1] Everyday literacy, however, was also used in the ways that individuals made decisions in social fields separate from the public life of the town. Successful players used multiple literacies to negotiate a variety of settings.

Bingo at Holy Cross "BINGO!" a voice cried out from across the room. My friend made an unintelligible sound as she pushed away from the table and threw her ink dabber down.[2] "That Shirley again," she said, shaking her head, "the third time this month." I asked her how she knew, and she laughed and said that if you played bingo with the same people long enough, you'd know all their voices and the way they yelled. In between games and between calls, the women at my table chatted and traded stories about friends and neighbors. Asking about one another's health, the health of a family member, or the job prospects of an unemployed friend, they kept up-to-date on the activities of the people they knew.

We were in a parish hall where a bingo game is held every Sunday night, and most of the participants are regulars. My friend also played at a large game held in the Dominion sports center and at a neighborhood club. Part of a "circuit," these women (there are a few men playing, but the crowd is predominantly women) spent a considerable amount of time together on a weekly basis. The crowd was also predominantly working class—sharing the experiences of growing up in a company town. Separations of economic status, however, were not distinct as all of my respondents, regardless of income, were familiar with "bingo hall culture" and could tell of times they had participated as teens or with relatives and friends.

The quality of information that was passed along during these Bingo conversations and in other exchanges between women over the phone and while visiting may seem mundane. Rarely did the conversation turn political unless they brought up local stories surrounding a hometown candidate. Rarely did the conversation turn to economics unless discussing a sale or the increase in prices at a particular store. Men's conversations conducted at local coffee shops and around kitchen tables were not much different except that economic talk included work, types of work in local contexts, local politics, and, of course, sports. Neither group tended to discuss the place of the local economy in a global or even national context. The acquisition of knowledge in local settings followed narrow courses of conversation, but these courses were very deep.

The knowledge individuals held about family members, employment histories, health records, and relationships was generations thick. Almost any story was accompanied by a recitation of names, clarification of "which John was that?" and references to places and events which provided context for both the listener and the teller. The women at my table kept up a running conversation which I had a difficult time following. It was like a murmur, *soto voce*, a litany of names with few explanations, which flowed without punctuation throughout the evening. Their conversation seemed so old that it no longer needed explanations or even enunciation. Regional comedians have made fun of the Cape Breton custom of asking strangers, "Who's your father?" to situate the newcomer within the network of Cape Breton families, but in the context of the rich texture of local narrative, such relationships were important to following such conversational streams.

Down at the Coffee Shop Other pockets of conversation expanded upon local ways of conversation, through discussion of "outside" events or information. One place these discussions could be heard was at local coffee shops, particularly the Tim Horton's on Commercial Street. Some of these conversations concerned the television-viewing practices of a group of unemployed or partially employed men who were regulars in the restaurant. On one occasion, I sat down with my coffee to hear a vehement argument from the man sitting behind me that Tyrannosaurus Rex did not have teeth. "But of course he does," his companion argued back. I must have turned around in surprise because the group of men talking smiled sheepishly and explained they were arguing about a show some of them had seen the night before on the Discovery Channel. I asked them if they watched that channel often and they emphatically agreed. "That's a great one," one man said, "lots of good stuff on that one." Another man interrupted, "But we have to try to get them to add the History Channel too. Then we'd really be set." This conversation was not typical for the morning crowd at Tim Horton's, nor was it typical for the coffee shop tucked under the dentist's office complex down the street, the Tim Horton's at Sterling Mall across town, nor Lilly's Restaurant on Brookside, where the mayor at that time ate his breakfast. It was not, however, unlikely. I observed many coffee shop conversations enjoy a spin around a new or unusual topic, if provided.

My being from the United States often started these conversations. "What do you think about gun control," someone would ask when they heard I was from the States. My lack of knowledge about gun control and a number of other "American" issues usually disappointed them. I did notice, however, in some of these conversations, that these arguments would become circular until someone interjected new information from a nonlocal source. Unless someone else was able to verify the new data, the conversation would dwindle off. One resident who had lived off-island for over ten years and returned to teach at the university defended this practice. "Local 'ignorance' is not ignorance," he said, "but a limited flow of information." He did admit that an increase in the flow of information (like the introduction of cable info-channels), however, does not necessitate an increase in analysis, especially when new information is not based or built upon local knowledge.

Sometimes news about Canada as a whole would get mixed up with information about the United States or other international politics. These misinterpretations were often provided as evidence of the negative aspects of living off-island. For example, one of my neighbors tried to engage me in a conversation about the dangers of allowing immigrants to come to Canada. There had been very few new residents moving to Glace Bay; in fact, one school official told me that they had enrolled only one new child from outside the Cape Breton School District between 1990 and 1995. Immigration then, into this region of Canada from abroad, was an area in which local residents had very little personal experience. The news broadcasts received in Glace Bay from Detroit cable stations included reports regarding immigration and the problems of ethnic tensions in border regions of the South and Southwest of the United States. My friend argued with me that "they were pouring in" and that the hard-earned money of Canadians was being spent on social services and health care for a bunch of "Spanish-speaking foreigners." I asked where he had heard of these problems and whom he meant by "them" and he told me it was on the news. "Everybody knows about this," he said, "but the government just keeps letting it happen." I tried clarifying that I knew it would be very difficult for *me* to immigrate to Canada and that Canadian immigration laws were very strict. I tried suggesting that perhaps the news reports he was hearing were regarding the controversy over immigration regulations in California and Texas. "No," he said bitterly, "it's all those people in Ottawa that are letting them in and spending all that money." Granted, Canada does have difficulties, as do all industrial nations, in trying to find equitable ways of assisting new immigrants. Perhaps this man was fully knowledgeable about these efforts. His arguments, however, seemed to mix information about the United States with information about Toronto and other urban "problem areas."

A local community service worker told me that the choice of cable television provider made a difference in the usefulness of television for local analysis of regional problems. "They used to use a company out of Bangor," she explained. The Bangor stations, including local news about the coastal towns of Maine, related more directly to issues of interest to the Maritime residents of Canada. The Detroit stations, she went on to say, have more violence than local viewers were used to seeing. She also complained about the loss of the local programming from Maine that would show stories about fishing, agriculture, and traditional music. "We just have more in common with people in Maine than we do with people in Detroit and Toronto." Ironically, in the 1990s the people of Glace Bay had a great deal in common with the people in both regions: the maritime regions of New England and the deindustrializing sections of central Canada held conditions similar to those in Glace Bay. What this woman's comment might indicate is that the "simple" life of rural and coastal Maine matched the narrative of local identity more closely than the "modern" life of Toronto and Detroit. Glace Bay residents' responses to television reflected more than just a rural/urban dichotomy; their interpretations matched the representations of the outside world and of themselves that seemed to fit their sensibilities best.

Caledonia Dart League Similar to the familiarity of the coffee shop and the Bingo game, weekly darts leagues provide opportunities for town residents to strengthen their community connections while enjoying one another's company. Most neighborhoods, especially those historically connected to a mine, had a social or sporting club. Almost identical to one another, these clubs usually consisted of a large room with dartboards regularly spaced along one or more walls and long, bare folding tables and surrounded by chairs. Separated from the main room, there was usually a small kitchenette connected by an open window counter, which also served as a bar. In some cases the bar would have a separate smaller window. Some clubs also had a separate "pub" room as well. Social halls like these can be found in community clubs and fraternal organizations across North America.

At the Caledonia Ladies Dart League, which played at the Caledonia Club on Pitt Street, the group was divided into teams at the beginning of the season, and they played, round-robin fashion, each week against a different team. At the end of the season they had playoffs, and winning teams were awarded prizes. Although all of this seems quite ordinary, during my observations, play frequently overlapped with networking, and levels of "local literacy" were often expressed in the relationships of players to one another. Leaders were chosen for their skill and knowledge of the game as well as their social connections. Certain players were respected for their ability to keep score quickly (requiring quick mental math skills), and sometimes those who were in school (especially university) were teased if they made mistakes. Conversations usually concentrated on family business—who was getting married, who was sick, who was having a baby, etc., but as spring approached, many conversations centered on upcoming graduations and plans for the future.

One of the women in the dart league worked as a low-level manager for a government office in Sydney. Her participation in conversations around the table consisted of everything but her job, but when she scored a double[3] and led her team to victory, she would slap herself on the back in congratulations. Her success was part of her self-confidence. Her knowledge about her capabilities was understood by the group, reinforced in her own mind with each well-placed dart, and taken back to her job and her family. In more private conversations, she talked about going on trips for job training and her advancement within her division, verbally patting herself on the back as she described her success and tried to alleviate the anxiety she felt about entering new fields of knowledge. For this woman, the two worlds of work and play were separate, and yet the multiple literacies she used to negotiate one served her in the other as well.

Many of the players were related. There were some mother/daughter groups and lots of sisters and cousins. They caught up on family news but more often passed on information to extended families and neighbors. Often these conversations included exchanging resources or making arrangements for future trades. For example, preparing a daughter for graduation was an expensive enterprise because getting ready included finding dresses for both the senior prom and graduation. Both mother and daughter took these decisions seriously and sought out as much information as possible about buying used dresses, finding resources for fabric or sale price clothing within the region, and trading skills and services in the form of sewing or cleaning. Sometimes conversations related to employment when individuals asked probing questions about another person's family member's new job or lay-off, searching for clues about possible openings or potential job loss for their own family.

The ability to do this sort of information exchange and probing well was a learned skill. I discovered this quickly through reactions to my own questioning and probing. Although an outsider, if I followed the unwritten local script of questioning, individuals would often play along, answering my questions as they would a neighbor's. If I stepped over the line, by asking a question too close to an economic source, for example, they would shut down, and others who were listening would let me know by their body language and change of topic that I had overstepped.

One example of this occurred when I asked one of the team members at my table about her son's new job. She had just finished reporting on his "gettin' on" at a local business, so I thought the topic was fair game. I knew he had been working through the unemployment office, so I asked if they had helped in getting the position. The woman ignored my question, and someone else changed the subject. Later, when we were leaving the building, she told me that her brother-in-law had helped his nephew, but that those kinds of connections "shouldn't be talked about in public." I was confused by this revelation. People spoke of connections all the time and openly suggested that connections have been used when they heard of someone's success. Information was often bartered, however, and my probing offered the woman no benefits in exchange for her information.

Although sharing local wisdom took place predominantly within local contexts, connections could reach across the country. For example, when trying to find curtains to match her wallpaper trim, one woman mentioned her problem at the darts table. Her sister-in-law mentioned finding curtains at a local store. The next week, after looking locally, the curtains still hadn't been found. By this point, relatives in Ontario had been told of the problem and passed back information about availability of curtains there. A sample of the wallpaper was sent west with another relative heading to visit in the Toronto area. By the end of the month, the matching curtains had been found, purchased, and sent back to Cape Breton. Although a complicated process overall, the pure volume of conversation about these drapes was overwhelming. Again, the acquisition and passing on of information was a thick process in Glace Bay, with many layers of relationships and practices of communication.

Coffee Shop Networking With scarce jobs creating a difficult or temporary employment market, individuals bartered services, products, and information in an underground economy. Household economies were frugal and inventive—no one shopped a sale better than a Glace Bay woman. Part-time work or under-the-table jobs were brokered through complex systems of family and political networking. Local literacy—the ability to understand and communicate information successfully on an everyday basis—was crucial to surviving in this close-knit community. In pursuing educational credentials, there was a difference between developing skills for work and developing knowledge that could lead to decision-making in a local context. Local residents were aware of this difference.

For example, in telling his story about returning to Glace Bay to live after years of working as an engineer abroad and in western Canada, John told me of his repeated experiences with formal education. At the same time he told the story of his negotiation of local networks of employment in the town. Unemployed off and on since his return, John had also worked as an instructor at UCCB, as a crew leader on a grant project, and as a laborer. He had participated in short-term training programs as well. All of these experiences were a product of what he called his political savvy as well as his educational achievements. In the course of our conversation, he also mentioned wanting to return to school to complete a degree that would allow him to work in social services. "That's where the good jobs are," he said, "and I'd be able to use my smarts to help people like myself."

To show me what this process was like, he invited me to go along with him to apply for a job. He picked me up at the coffee shop and we drove into Sydney. Along the way, he filled out an employment application, writing on the dashboard at stoplights, all the while telling me how this "works." "You've got to know somebody," he said. "I know a guy down at this office and if I hand him my application directly, I'll have a better chance at getting the job." I asked him how he heard about the opening. "That's just it," he said, "I heard about them hiring more people through another friend." He told me that timing was important because sometimes rumors fizzled out even if there had been some work available, and other times, if you applied too soon, you'd lose out along the way. We parked in front of a small government building I'd never seen before and John went in with his application. He came right out and said, "Now we wait. I should know in about a week."

A few weeks later, John told me he had been given the job as a supervisor of a construction project down on the harbor front. I learned, through listening to conversations between John and his friends at the coffee shop (where he still spends most of his time despite his new job) and trying to follow along with their joking, that John's job consisted of showing up at the foreman's trailer in the morning, handing out work assignments, and then checking on the work crew later in the day. Although his friends respected John's engineering and management experience, they kidded him about the everyday activities that the job required. John defended himself, saying he didn't really have to be there the whole time, and, since the harbor was only a few hundred feet away from the coffee shop, his crew knew where to find him. I also learned that, although the job was short-lived, John would get enough stamps to make unemployment again in six months, and he told me that he was doing what he could to make sure his crew would make it too. "Sometimes that means giving a longer assignment to somebody who needs more stamps," he said. "I try to take care of them." The short-term nature of such work required thinking ahead to times of unemployment.

I asked John if his education was important to him and if it had helped him get this job. "Oh, learning's important all right," he said, "but you've got to learn to play the game too. It's who you know not what you know." I pressed him to elaborate on the value of his formal education. He described setting up an engineering course at UCCB. He tried to develop the curriculum, he said, to allow students to apply their knowledge as much as possible and use a network of contacts. It was important to the program, he continued, to provide the trainees not only with the technical skills but also with the experience and connections that would help them get jobs. I asked why he was not still teaching and he shook his head, "I didn't have the degree you know, plus I wouldn't play politics so they forced me out." John explained that the administration wanted him to accept certain people into the program, people who had connections with the political party in power. He said he would not do it, so they moved the program to Halifax, which made it difficult for him to continue. John preferred to be loyal to his local network rather than "play politics" at the provincial level.

John's story reflects his interpretation of the intricate network of contacts, experience, and "savvy" that were required to manipulate the government system of unemployment insurance and grant work in Glace Bay at the time. This local wisdom was crucial to achieving "success" as locally defined. John could leave town and get another engineering job, but he said he had spent too much time away from home and he and his wife wanted to be near their families. His "local literacy" allowed him to parlay his technical expertise into jobs, albeit low-paying ones. This seemed to be enough for him as the town itself provided many of the perks that a higher-paying job elsewhere would not. John was active in his church; he enjoyed the camaraderie of meeting with his friends a few nights a week, and he relished in the laid-back lifestyle that his Glace Bay life afforded him. When he occasionally sounded regretful, it was with regard to formal education, where he saw the credentials that would give him options his current "smarts" could not provide.

These examples show just some of the many contexts in which residents of Glace Bay demonstrated their local literacy. Becoming an "educated person" in local contexts required the application of strategies of local knowledge acquisition and production as well as formal practices of schooling. Methods of acquiring knowledge and skills, therefore, were not constrained to school or training, nor were they limited to a particular social class or cultural group. Local residents of all occupations and various economic resources also sought out and developed resources for self-improvement.

Applying Local Wisdom: Decision-Making
Educated individuals from "away" who work with the people of Glace Bay often mentioned how "childlike" they are. If this were an earlier time and a different political climate, I would not have been surprised to hear the description "primitive." This recalls Geertz's (1983) explanation of how social scientists have tried to straighten out the convoluted lines of everyday life in traditional societies to find the formal paths that are natural to political and economic theory. Cape Bretoners, like any group, do not function in straight lines. It is in the complexity of lived experiences that individuals make decisions and create strategies for survival. If we embrace this approach, then it becomes easier to understand why forty-year-old fishermen dislike "life skills development classes." It becomes easier to understand why, when confronted constantly by stories of friends who have gone away and found the "outside" cold, a folk image of the closeness and solidarity of the community is maintained and defended.

Getting a Good Bargain On any given morning in Glace Bay you can stand in most shop lineups or in a corner of a coffee shop and listen to women compare prices. In my interviews they also explained how they had agonized over this decision or that. Although family responsibilities often tied individuals, especially women, to Glace Bay, families also provide a space in which to demonstrate decision-making abilities. Many of the government officials and business leaders I talked to spoke of the lack of decision-making ability of the local people, but one woman I spoke with carefully explained how her mother and then herself had made all the everyday decisions in the household. They decided how the meager household budget was to be spent, who would get what material possessions, which child would go where for what type of education or job opportunity. This comment surprised me and I asked whether the element of active decision-making was perhaps hidden in the home so outsiders wouldn't see how carefully people were making strategies to survive. She emphatically agreed.

For example, another woman described how she used her experiences in finding work to help her guide her daughter's choices regarding education. Her teenage daughter was enrolled in a French immersion program that was widely talked about as being for the "better" students and which would offer many opportunities because of Canada's bilingual government policies. Through her own experiences—a failed marriage and a lost career—the woman said she had learned about how to take opportunities and be aggressive about following dreams. Living in Glace Bay, she was able to afford to buy a company house from a relative for a reasonable price. She used her sense of design developed while living in Halifax and Montreal to renovate her home and provide a comfortable and safe space in which to raise her daughter. She felt confident and empowered by her daughter's success in school and her own abilities to seek out information to help make decisions about her family's future.

Another woman was pursuing her own degree at UCCB. She had two children and had had to accept welfare in order to get by while a student but described herself as being in control of her own destiny. Her graduation in May of 1995 marked the start of a new life away from Glace Bay in Ontario. She had returned home in order to receive the support of her family (and of the government) but planned on leaving with her new educational credentials. She explained her rationale for accepting assistance:

> I don't like taking assistance, but there was no other way. I had to do something for myself, for my children. My family understands. Being on assistance doesn't carry as much shame for women. They help out when they can, watching the children. But with my school schedule, I can do most of it myself.

In making decisions regarding their own education and that of their children, these women discussed with me their sense of accomplishment and wisdom. One woman said, "I may not always make the right decision, but I do the best that I can and I learn from my mistakes." Social networks provided support, but most of the women I spoke with also referred to their own learning experiences either in gathering resources (enrolling a child in a special program, preparing a dossier to apply for jobs) or learning from their own trials and errors. These examples demonstrate that women in Glace Bay have held a strong sense of personal efficacy in the realm of household decision-making. In many ways, this confidence was expressed as they made economic decisions about their schooling and employment despite officials' comments about local residents' passivity toward their futures.

Navigating the World of Politics Comments by government officials, even those who lived in Glace Bay, often centered around the inability of local residents to participate actively in decision-making processes. Although I did hear a great deal of apathy with regard to local politics, especially with regard to the power held by Ottawa and Halifax, I was impressed by the number of people who held very strong opinions about the future of the town, although they rarely expressed them in positive or proactive ways. When I asked specifically about local politics, many people suggested I speak with local labor leaders, indicating a continuing perception that change comes through the union rather than individuals.

Herbie Nash was one such leader (retired by the time of our conversation) whose house sat on the corner of the turnaround by Fisherman's Beach. Herbie was very active in the in-shore fishermen's union. He, like many Glace Bay residents, had very little respect for the wisdom of politicians and bureaucrats. He told a story about the time he went to Ottawa to talk to the federal fisheries minister, and the workers in the fisheries department did not know where the minister's office was. "They don't know nothing about it," he said. "I suppose they didn't know what to do with me, dressed like a fisherman and all."

The view out over the ocean from Herbie's house was beautiful. Surrounding the town and yet often just out of sight, the ocean at the end of the street and its reflection in the blue-gray skies above town were physical reminders of the marginalized nature of Glace Bay as a political entity. The decisions came from Ottawa with very little local input. When I asked Herbie to tell me about how unemployment insurance (UI) had affected the fishermen, he was not sure how to answer. "I don't really know," he said, and I asked him instead to explain recent events in history of the industry.

He explained that, when the fish population went down, the fishermen became dependent on the UI in the off season. In 1979, he continued, the government kicked the in-shore fishermen out of the gulf, and the off-shore draggers went to Ft. Vieux and hurt the spawning grounds by harvesting too many juvenile fish. From 1983 to 1987, he explained, 65 percent of the juveniles were caught and destroyed. "This basically killed the industry," Herbie finished.

After a long pause of silence, staring into his tea, Herbie offered an alternative solution to the government downsizing affected by closing the fishing grounds to in-shore fishermen:

> If they [the government] wanted to eliminate 50 percent of the fishing population, all they have to do is eliminate the off-shore draggers and that would eliminate their crews, the people who work in the plant, and a variety of other guys. It would also return control of the fisheries to the independent competition of in-shore fishermen; they can't do the damage the draggers do with their technology.

He admitted, however, difficulties with this plan:

> Fishermen are hard to organize. They're independent, but they're dependent on the fish, and on the markets, so it's difficult to say what will happen.

Once Herbie started to share his knowledge of the industry with me, he was verbose. Without hedging or avoiding questions, he explained clearly and eloquently his views of what had happened to the fishing industry and how the problem might be addressed. Once given a local context in which to work, Herbie's analytical skills proved to be more than adequate to the task of explaining his position on a complicated issue.

In response to my question about how Ottawa would respond to his ideas, Herbie was emphatic:

> Take the politics out of it! Train the fishermen to give them a greater voice. The government needs to be more honest with the fishermen...telling them the truth in time for them to act upon it.

The quality of information available was identified as the key to the quality of decision-making possible.

Education is important, Herbie went on; "Now you have to have an education only to put up with the bureaucrats." He described how the unions were trying to work together to provide training programs themselves in communications and in co-management. The government was interested in communications, he said, but was trying to avoid co-management. "The key," he continued, "is getting the information to the communities and giving them the skills to know what to do with it other than bitch to one another." The local programs included trying to use computers and an Internet linkup as well as video. Herbie finished, "They're bringing back the pony express in order to save themselves." I looked around Herbie's kitchen table, littered with faxes, government documents, and correspondence. "Your table looks like my office at the university," I joked with him. "Yeah," he smiled, "I guess you could say I'm getting a degree in bureaucracy!"

Multiple Literacies: Insiders and Outsiders
It is important to stress that local networks like those that the women playing Bingo or the unemployed negotiate were not the only networks in Glace Bay, nor were local forms of knowledge the only form of literacy practiced by residents of the town. To assume so would be to oversimplify the practices of knowledge acquisition and transmission within the town and to overlook differences as they were played out in dialogue and actions. Individuals maintained their distinct locations within the net, and those distinctions changed depending on the context. For example, when one of my neighbors spoke about the curtains or floors in her house, she would often refer to "my floors, my curtains" in the same way that she would identify a family member, remotely related, as "my brother's sister's cousin." Labeling this cousin as family was not the same as calling her a friend; the two categories were distinct. And yet, because a family member, however remote, was an acceptable role, recognizing that relationship helped maintain the stability of the community network by emphasizing the familiar rather than strange, thus implying a certain friendliness that may not have existed. People who come from off-island often did not fit this system of recognition, nor did people who embraced the values of the outside or strange over the local or familiar. People who did not play the game, who did not use the complex codes of local networking, caused dissonance for the group but more likely for themselves.

I found that when individuals described themselves as feeling like "outsiders," it was often in cases where their personal search for information had led them far afield of what was shared locally on a regular basis. In instances of such marginalization (the status of being or feeling different), how was that difference handled? What references of learning were called upon, and when, if ever, was formal education used? For example, in two separate conversations with two older women, I heard completely different interpretations of a Christmas concert shown on television. One woman complained that the singers should have "worn something bright" and that it was a shame the show turned out so dreary. The other woman commented on the elegance of the singers' black velvet gowns and how nice it was to have "a real concert" to watch. The two "readings" of the television program may reflect differences of class, although the two women shared the same economic, religious, ethnic, and social background. The comments do reveal differences of personal taste that are difficult to attribute. In their learning histories, however, the two women's educational paths may explain a great deal about their interpretive frameworks.

The woman who complained about the lack of color in the show was very social. She had a grade nine education and did not pursue formal education after leaving school. She did not read a great deal but liked to go to public events—concerts, shows, movies, and, of course, Bingo. Her daily conversations included an amazing array of information that was exchanged, told, and retold again and again—each time with new analysis and later referred to as new information was introduced. Her conversations with her family and friends were a constant confirmation of her life. She took in information, related it to herself, packaged it in neat bundles, and put it away, as neatly as she put away her material goods in her houses. Information, however, did not always fit, as in some of the questions I asked, and was then discarded or critiqued as being "wrong."

In comparison, the woman who enjoyed the elegance of the concert also had a grade nine education, but frequently participated in community-sponsored courses in painting and drawing since leaving school. She read a great deal and talked of her father, a coal miner, giving her "the classics" as a child. She also enjoyed going to public events but was more likely to go to a lecture at the university than a bingo game. When I asked if she felt that concerts like the one on television would be popular in Glace Bay, she said, "Probably not. They like folksy entertainment here." Although she was an active member of the community, she admitted that her tastes were different from those of others in town. Which of these women was more "local"? I would suggest that they were both equally fixed in local ways of knowing. Multiple readings of local narratives and practices might also be thought of as multiple literacies rather than oppositional ones as local residents searched for ethnographic alternatives of interpreting Glace Bay life.

Shared knowledge that is familiar and within the context of frameworks constructed over time through "deep" courses of conversation was "public" in the sense that the information is accessible and typical. When someone invested in contest discourse within the town of Glace Bay, it was not by starting an argument or challenging another speaker (acceptable forms of conversation). Rather, they did so by marginalizing themselves from the "everydayness" of daily exchange as I might have done when I asked analytical questions out of context or as some of the women who I describe below might have done when they sought out "intellectual" conversations. In such cases they may have been using a kind of global literacy, a knowledge system which was successful in fields outside of Glace Bay but not in local "public" discourse. Personalized learning like that contained in some of my research questions and in individuals' comments about their own education was often not read as group oriented and therefore not local or, in many ways, practical. Intellectual conversation or dialogue which was informed by the analysis of information by the speaker separate from locally shared knowledge was not public in that it was derived from private and therefore inaccessible sources which defied local categories.

One morning when my landlady and I were having our morning tea, I joked with her that my school language was not very useful in talking in Glace Bay. She did not agree directly, but she smiled and changed the subject in a way that told me, again, that a meta-conversation about language was not what she considered a useful conversation. In talking to other people in town, however, especially those who had been to university, I made similar comments and they often agreed, citing the narrowness of Glace Bay thinking and the absence of analysis in ways that people talk. I often had to ask to whom they were referring when they talked of "Glace Bay" thinking—were they not members of the community themselves? The dichotomy of "local" versus "away" was raised in this manner again and again. By acquiring a university education, necessarily "away," these speakers had a reflexive position within the town which sometimes marginalized them by including an "outside looking in" kind of perspective.

When conducting life history interviews with older residents, however, many of the seniors spoke nostalgically about a time when conversation and the exchange of ideas were more "exciting." "People's communication skills were better then than now," one older man told me. These comments contained the same kind of critique as those of middle-aged university graduates but were based on the passage of time within the town rather than new perspectives brought back from the outside world. Changes in the town therefore reflected changes in perspectives about learning and knowledge.

Conversations in Glace Bay were not all based on "public" knowledge. Some people actively sought out conversations in which they could share the information they had gained from private exploration, reading and otherwise, conversations that might not have appealed to just anyone in the town but which provided informal learning opportunities for smaller groups with similar interests. Opportunities to share in this way, however, had declined. Many people with whom I spoke no longer belonged to as many community organizations, and the practice of general reading seemed to be diminished, as it has been throughout modern society, by the presence of television.

Engaging in an internal dialogue with outside sources such as reading, listening to the radio, or watching television, however, were still described by many residents, especially women, as being part of what they considered to be a successful and satisfying life. These practices alone were not enough to marginalize a person, but engaging in sources which require knowledge of nonlocal information may have felt isolating. This was especially true for women who, for whatever reasons, were still living in Glace Bay but would have liked to be part of a larger network outside the region. The ways that they established these contacts were multiple. One woman regularly read national newspapers and, as part of her professional development, read trade materials in her field. Another woman listened to the CBC radio station, including local programs, national news, and weekend "magazines." Yet another woman was actively pursuing a course in theological study, following a self-directed curriculum of reading and essay assignments. All of these women mentioned to me that they wished they had people to "talk to" in Glace Bay about their ideas and thoughts.

The fact that the individuals I describe here are predominantly women may be a result of my being a woman and the fact that I found it easier and more socially convenient to establish rapport with women than with men. I did hear of similar self-exploration from a few men, but most of them were retired or on long-term disability. As I suggested earlier, the experiences of these women may reflect tensions experienced by a number of people within the town who had the potential to be economically or socially mobile and yet were also loyal to a sense of belonging in the town. It was more likely that men, if they had similar interests in exploring new ideas or connections, would have followed those inclinations away from the region. Most of the women I spoke with continued to live in Glace Bay because of strong family ties or a lack of resources to live elsewhere with the same comfort level and support structure. Even while seeking out nonlocal resources for themselves, each woman expressed contentment with many facets of her life. Despite the lack of "conversation," they were happy living in Glace Bay, at least for now. One woman remarked:

> I never really thought that there was anything bad about Glace Bay, I just wanted to see the world. Now that I've come back, I love just being with the people...like the old people down at the club playing cards....But it wasn't until I moved back that I started to notice things? Like, I wouldn't say they were narrow-minded, but maybe locally focused? Yes, they do make comments without knowing all the facts, but I didn't notice it growing up.

What was remarkable about this group of people and their desire for more fulfilling conversation in the town was the incongruence between the wish for more talk amidst the overwhelming amount of talk that went on in the town! One woman explained this contradiction in describing local "talk," "It's not dialogue—the kind that promotes growth. If you want to be one of them, you've got to talk about what interests them—daily life—it's not the issues." Again, the extremely local nature of most dialogue was emphasized.

Because of the nature of my questions and the perspective I brought as both an outsider and a social scientist, my conversations with these women tended to focus on their interpretations of the town and its future. With one friend, for example, we talked often and at length about the development possibilities of her small craft business. With another, we discussed the future of the town in terms of unemployment and the possibilities for those who were currently dependent on social assistance to find employment and become self-sufficient. Within these conversations, these women made insightful comments about their town. Their own place in the town was ambiguous as they sometimes felt isolated but at other times comforted by their families and neighbors. One woman's ambiguity stemmed from her lack of family—as an orphan she had moved from home to home. She described herself as self-sufficient and explained that is why she continues to seek out knowledge. These ambiguities were reflected in the women's perspectives of the town's future, bemoaning the lack of initiative of the townspeople to pursue effective development strategies but at the same time pointing out the ways in which the town was successful—that it was a nice place to live.

Authority and Expertise: The Limits of Local Literacy
Economic practices defined as the informal economy do not require formal education, but can be implemented in any setting where there is enough local knowledge to communicate a solution. For example, while waiting in line to use a computer at the university, I was cut off by a young woman who took the next available seat. I told her I had been waiting for the computer and that I was next in line and she looked astonished. "Don't you have a friend?" she asked, implying that I should have known to negotiate the use of a computer with someone I knew. UCCB students implemented their "informal economy" in school in a variety of ways to accomplish academic tasks or to make extra money while on vacation. Getting time on a school computer, for example, or sharing the purchase of books were some of the ways students use community resources for academic success. Overall, however, the bartering of information through community networks was antithetical to what was often a one-way path of information typical of a merit-based educational system. Success in school, as in transnational markets of employment, seldom benefits solely from the use of negotiated networks because of the academic authority of credentials. The issue of authority in knowledge transmission and reception was found in other settings as well.

For example, I went with an older friend to the hospital to visit her brother, who was very ill. My friend was a leader in her social circle and the head of her family. In talking with the doctor, however, she spoke like a child. "Yes sir, " she said dutifully in a way I had never heard her speak before. In the course of the conversation the doctor told her that she would need to inform the rest of the family about their relative's condition. She clung to this instruction for the following weeks, telling each family member, in turn, that she was in charge, that she would let them know what was going on. Later, when her brother died, she was frustrated by the legal ambiguities about her status as next of kin. She was his closest relative; he had lived with her for some time, and his children who lived away were unfamiliar to her.

When I spoke with her a few weeks later, she told me with unusual pique that "they" had said his ex-wife would be "before her in line if there was anything to be had." I knew her irritation had nothing to do with inheritance, especially since there would be little to gain, but with the uncertainty with her legal status. Although this woman was a genius at unraveling complicated kinship relationships in social settings, her lack of understanding of legal and business transactions frustrated her and caused her a great deal of anxiety. Fortunately, one of her brother's children came to visit and awarded her the deference she felt was due to her as head of the household. She seemed much happier in the weeks that followed, helping her young relative make the necessary connections to settle her father's business.

The controversy over the consolidation of health care facilities in the region also raised questions of authority and expertise. During the early 1990s, a new regional hospital was built just outside of Sydney. After it was finished, the other hospitals in the area were restructured to make use of shared resources. St. Joseph's, the oldest hospital in Glace Bay and the one to which older Catholic residents still used exclusively, effectively was closed except for its long-term care facilities. Although patients would still go to St. Joseph's for treatment, they would often be sent to Glace Bay General, the community hospital to get tests or other treatments. These decisions created a great deal of controversy in the town, especially for older patients, who felt they were getting pushed around. One local nurse argued that the people in the town were misguided in their complaints. She said, "Just because you have a hospital doesn't mean you have adequate health care." She went on to describe the deficiencies in the local facilities and the benefits of the regional hospital. Her authority regarding the pros and cons of the health care policy decisions was based on her expertise as a nurse and as a health care administrator. Like other nurses and health care practitioners in the town, however, her expertise was derived from her professional training and work experience rather than local sources of shared knowledge. The controversy over health care, therefore, was locally perceived as a contest between local control and external authority, despite the fact that the community had its own sources of expertise that supported the regional institution.

While visiting a social service office, I was also struck by the passive reactions of local residents to what they perceived as outside decision-making. While sitting in the waiting area, I noticed the silence. In a town where almost all public spaces were full of conversation, the waiting room was deathly quiet. It was almost like being in a doctor's office, and I wondered, "Are we here for treatment?" I asked John MacEachern, a local politician, why he thought the people receiving assistance were so quiet. He replied that although the coal company was gone, the sense of decision-making coming "from away" was still there:

> Before you would never go to the company and demand something. You'd work together to fight for changes, but individuals wouldn't do it on their own even though they were dependent on them.

His reference to the labor struggles was interesting. Tom Miller, the curator at the Miners' Museum, made a similar comment about the changes in local activism from the early days:

> In the early days, the average man was encouraged to educate himself so that he could "speak" at the same level as the owners and managers. There was the assumption that the worker was downtrodden because of ignorance. Once the UMW gained a more powerful position, the drive for education waned off.

He went on to explain that the need for a local voice against outside voices seemed to have diminished. Although there were people who acted as watchdogs for the community (the health care controversy mentioned above is a good example), local residents were more likely to let a few people do the work for them rather than rally together.

People did not seem to use local literacies to communicate with one another and develop common issues upon which the community could make decisions. John MacEachern said, in irritation, about his constituency:

> Even though we are dependent on the government, people demand certain services as their rights. They don't seem to realize where the money comes from....Instead of sharing what's available, the people try to take what others have...get your piece before it's gone. But then it's gone too fast. We've exhausted what we had.

The practice of "taking what you can get" and competing with your neighbor for scarce resources seemed to have replaced communal practices of solidarity despite the "folk" myth of community presented in narrative conventions of creation myths and booster tales. Miller described this competition:

> Now there's a feeling that's different from the American myth of keeping up with the Jones. Rather than keeping up, it's a matter of tearing down. People don't want to support their own. In order to make it here, you have to work twice as hard and face jealousy. If you leave and make it and come back, they welcome your success with open arms...but you can't do it here.

Perhaps the downside of a myth of solidarity is that when resources are unequally distributed, blame must be put on those who have worked their way to the top.

I asked a union organizer who lives in a rural fishing village an hour north of Glace Bay what he thought of the area's potential for sustainable development. In his rural community, the lobstermen had banded together to increase the recommended carapace size of lobsters caught in their traps. This resulted in catching more mature lobsters, reducing the overall catch but improving the health of the lobster grounds. In addition, this group had agreed on a plan to share lobstering areas so that all the participants in the group had a better chance at bringing in a fair catch. This aspect of the plan was particularly noteworthy as traditional fishing practices along this coast required that you fish the grounds directly adjacent to the land that you owned or leased. Both initiatives were developed within the local group with the help of their union organizers. Both initiatives contradicted traditional practices of lobstering as well as traditional rules of territorial rights. They may, however, eventually save the livelihood of their community.

I raise this example because, in contrast to the inshore fishermen and fish plant workers in Glace Bay who had passively reacted to the government TAGS program, the lobstermen of St. Ann's Bay asked for government assistance in training to develop their organizational skills—how to run meetings effectively, how to set up better information networks, how to negotiate sensitive issues, etc.—rather than retraining for new trades. Fisheries workers, in general, had an advantage over individuals in other occupations, in that they were for the most part self-employed or part of very small crews. These fishermen, however, expressed a need for networking skills that went beyond their local practices of communication and the skills they used on the water.

What would it have taken for the Glace Bay fishing community to make proactive requests in response to the restructuring of the fisheries?

New class divisions within Glace Bay between those who come from educated families and those who do not may have made a difference as to whether the less-well-educated fishermen felt able to formulate a request so appropriate for their needs as these lobstermen did. People in Glace Bay with educational credentials were more likely to use their knowledge of the system and government to take advantage of the few opportunities available or to participate in entrepreneurial initiatives.

For example, a placement officer at one of the proprietary career schools revealed that she had worked in the Glace Bay fish plant. A good student in high school who did not continue her education because of the need to earn money for her family, this woman convinced her employment counselor to help her get funding for a university course in business management even though she had not yet been laid off. She completed that course while still working at the plant and was then able to apply for a small retraining grant that helped her buy clothes and pay for transportation so she could get her current job. Her educational success in the past gave this individual the confidence to navigate the government system and find a service position. Those for whom formal educational strategies were new, however, those who had depended on the government while waiting for previously lucrative industries to revive, or those who had only recently lost the revenues upon which they depended may not have been able to imagine themselves within the contexts of development strategies as yet not defined.

Similar to the days of street corner activism, local residents talked, listened, and read, but as was not the case in their successful labor battles, their understanding of information was often framed by negative local interpretations that diminished the power of their thinking for action. The people of the town were proud of their labor history, that by coming together to meet and talk and share ideas they had been able to create something that could work for them. The practice of gathering together to share and critique information continued, but it rarely seemed to affect local residents' relationships with institutions and organizations outside of the town as their criticism was sweeping and rarely included solutions or concrete requests. Still fighting against a company that no longer existed and dependent on a government they did not trust, they either did not have the political literacy skills to understand global and national politics or chose not to engage in them. After decades of being powerless to affect the decision-making process, they often did nothing but criticize the decisions that were made. Dan Monroe, former mayor of Glace Bay, described the town as "a place of survivors not winners."

Conclusion

The ability to access, assimilate, and use information to build local knowledge was dependent on a number of factors. Local residents engaged in multiple practices of literacy, whether following the deep course of local wisdom regarding family and everyday life or introducing new information through independent reading or school learning. The ways that information was used, however, were restricted by applicability to perceived needs. My analytic questions held little value for my landlady or her friends at bingo. Yet, in conversations with other residents, my questions allowed them to talk of their own ethnographic analysis of their town and to express some of the discomfort they felt in the marginalizing practices of local talk. Information, however, in any form was necessary for effective decision-making.

Local literacies, knowledge of complex family networks, internal politics, household economies, and the ability to pull together in times of grief or tragedy were not capitalized on outside of these local settings. Although formal education provided credentials for work, it did not seem to link local survival strategies with those needed in an increasingly translocal world. Their history was rich and full of examples of community activism and survival, but an emphasis on individual advancement and meritocratic academic achievement seemed to undermine collaborative ambitions. "If you try to get ahead," one woman said, "they'll pull you down." Perhaps in order to understand and aid this community in crisis, it is less important to focus on improving formal literacy skills and vocational aptitudes (areas of knowledge that individuals already enthusiastically seek and gain) than to find ways to transfer local literacy skills and systems of communication such as gossip and barter into empowered forms of decision-making and community planning.

Notes

[1] Bourdieu's concept of cultural capital is often narrowly defined as those norms and practices that are most useful for negotiating middle-class institutions. His development of the notion of habitus, however, acknowledges that there are multiple forms of cultural capital. What was useful in the "field" of Glace Bay, however, may not be useful in the field of post-secondary education.

[2] Bingo playing cards were printed on newsprint sheets rather than cardboard cards. Players marked off their numbers by "dabbing" them with large sponge highlighter

pens called dabbers. A well-schooled bingo player's bag held dabbers, a glue stick for gluing together multiple sheets, candy or snacks, a deck of cards for a pregame with friends, and good luck tokens. Entering the hall, players bought the number of sheets they wanted to play for the regular games and then also picked up "specials," game sheets for special series such as splitting half the take with the house, or winning a preset jackpot. Members of the sponsoring club or church and high school students who received "tips" from the winners staffed the game. On one occasion I overheard a winner saying to one of these workers, "Here, put this in your college fund," and handed the boy a hundred-dollar bill.

3   Most of the dart leagues in Glace Bay played a game called 301 (sometimes 201 or 501). Play was begun by each team "getting a double" by scoring a dart in the second thin band from the center of the board on any numbered section. From that point on each player who threw "took off" points based on the numerical value of what was hit. Doubles and triples could be won by hitting the thin bands as well. When the team was close to zero, they had to hit another "double" to "finish," and the final deduction had to equal zero. For example, with a remaining score of 15 the team had to hit an odd number to even out the score and then hit a double (e.g., 15-3-double 6). In Glace Bay, this explanation would have been laughable, as it was truly local knowledge.

Chapter 6
Barbarians at the Gate

> *I'm a Cape Breton Barbarian.*
> *We all are, or didn't you know.*
> *I'm a hairy and scary one.*
> *Even the Mainlanders say it's so.*
> — "The Rise and Follies of Cape Breton"

Giddens (1994) describes the maintenance of tradition in late modern society as a kind of security blanket against radical doubt and the threat of violence (tangible and intangible). In asking the question, "How do traditions persist in the late modern world?" he asks that we take a second look at postmodern theoretical models of fragmentation and disunity for those instances of interdependence and sharing. Traditions, he argues, are an important site of articulating change in local communities even as they seem to disappear:

> The dissolution of the local community, such as it used to be, is not the same as the disappearance of local life or local practices. Place, however, becomes increasingly reshaped in terms of distant influences drawn upon in the local arena. Thus local customs that continue to exist tend to develop altered meanings. They become either relics or habits. (p. 101)

The development of these altered meanings occurs through the discursive articulation of tradition. In this way, Giddens emphasizes, tradition is not just about celebrating the past or maintaining status quo, but it is also employed in relations of power and therefore only persists when negotiated and defended amid "pluralistic and competing values."

For Glace Bay, the constant renewal of tradition was found in the telling and retelling of stories of the past, in the physical presence of the Miners' Museum, and, perhaps more negatively, in local residents' lack of enthusiasm for outside initiatives for change. Their emphasis on the past may have been a result, not of a pathological resistance to participating in "modern life," but of a reaction to the ambiguities of that life. By making a "relic" out of the mines and a living museum of the habits of mining life, local residents were able to construct a sense of security and continuity for themselves that was not static but constantly reinterpreted. Bodnar (1989) argues that public memory often unfolds in stories or "plots" which change as the relations between the tellers and the institutions of power with which they interact are transformed. The maintenance of tradition, of the interdependence of social bonds in the past is, as Giddens says, difficult. But it is also promising. Tradition is based on interdependency rather than individualism and therefore provides a way to consider the world in terms of constructed relationships rather than fragments.

Stories of contest between labor and the company were told through atemporal narratives that incorporated the early history of the town into the more recent past. These ideological constructions of the past reflect a dialectic of local autonomy and corporate power. The Glace Bay creation myth is a classic North American success story in which the disunity of the past was resolved through the creation of a strong local identity (Greenhouse, Yngvesson, and Engel, 1994). Not to be confused with a simple narrative of a shared past or a black-and-white case of labor versus capital, the creation myths of Glace Bay, like those of other industrial towns, include the negotiation of multiple dimensions of conflict and consensus in the past. These negotiations are discursive justifications which continue to be used to help residents face the ambiguities of the present (Giddens, 1994).

The residents of Glace Bay, however, were not all "in the same boat." While some crafts may have been well guided, others were left adrift. Some had successfully negotiated educational credentials that prepared them to compete, and some were displaced, clutching outdated skill sets learned both on the job and at school. Their children were equally at risk for having to move to find work as the local economy offered little opportunity. Still, despite obvious differences of economic success, residents of the town declined to acknowledge differences of class.

Perhaps the tension between the haves and the have-nots in Glace Bay is difficult to describe because there had not been a catalyzing event in the town upon which one could pinpoint conflict since the takeover of the coal and steel industries by the government in 1969 (Yngvesson, 1993). It was not clear how ready Glace Bay residents were to support current labor despite the heritage of solidarity. In fact, during my stay, there was a strike at one of the grocery stores. It went all but unmentioned for days although I asked people what they thought. "I won't cross the line," one woman said, but then later admitted that she had gone in the week before to get some things on sale. Public interpretations of the relationship of work and ownership had changed since the strikes of the early part of the century.

It was easier, in many ways, for the people of Glace Bay to claim a shared "folk" identity. Some people, however, were in a position to use that identity, whereas others were more likely subject to it. The ability to be a member of the community and to objectively view that membership as separate from one's personal identity was a valuable skill in a region where the commodification of heritage and of image was so important to the tourism market. In a conversation with a retired school teacher who had moved back to the area after living away for over thirty years, we talked about what he considered to be a lack of "aesthetic taste" on the part of many Glace Bay residents. His living room was decorated with Celtic designs, and his house by the sea was carefully maintained to "fit" into the seascape of a fishing village. He complained that others' lawn ornaments and automotive "projects" would deter tourists from coming. Where did his notion of what a Cape Breton yard should look like come from? Was it a product of his education, his thirty years of being "from" Cape Breton rather than living on the island, or both? Did his stories of a coal-mining heritage, the father and grandfather in the mines, mean the same thing as the stories told by individuals living in split-level houses behind their parent's company house?

The emphasis on a particular common sense, a specific way of doing things, may have a negative implication for the "folk" of Glace Bay. The ideology of the "simple life" does not fit easily into the competitive environment of a global economy. Although social change, a history of out-migration, especially of young adults, and an increasingly gloomy economic forecast make the maintenance of a local identity crucial for local survival and for the maintenance of transnational community networks, this colloquial emphasis on a common sense or "folk" way may be self-defeating. The image of the Cape Breton barbarians, created by the tourism industry in the 1930s, remains. But the simple life of the crofters has been replaced by the so-called "decadent life" of the unemployed welfare recipient. Without understanding the irony, Glace Bay residents will sarcastically joke about their abilities to work the "system" while at the same time reiterating their "clannishness."

A "folk" identity may serve to allow Glace Bay residents to resist negative changes in terms of postmodern alienation, but in doing so it reinforces the reproduction of industrial models of work rather than empowering residents to imagine new identities. As the town becomes more and more economically stratified, definitions of historical "habits and relics" also become more diverse. Middle-class members of the community are able to draw upon their Cape Breton "folk" identity as an emblem of regional pride. At the same time, however, other residents continue to live in the shadow of capitalism that darkens the image of the company town. What is heritage for some, an identity they may put on or take off arbitrarily, is still a way of life for others. In this respect, Glace Bay remains a living museum of industrial dependency.

Community *Ceilidh*

If not coal miners and if not fishermen, who were the residents of Glace Bay? The town itself, while full of warm-hearted people and an interesting industrial history, held little aesthetic appeal for tourists, but the commodification of heritage seemed to be one of the only commercial options left. Tourism played a large role in providing options to Glace Bay residents with regard to reimagining their working-class roots. They were able to define themselves in terms of historical heroism as fighters and survivors rather than victims of the economy. By narrativizing their coal-mining past and even trying to make it work for them economically, they were able to join the rest of Cape Breton in developing the island for tourism. Almost as living "brochures," they taught their history to the outside world. Mocking their heritage as "barbarians," they were able to enjoy the "good things" about life in Glace Bay: family, tradition, and good times.

Labels like "clannish" helped promote a positive image of a communal whole while still maintaining a hint of the untamable. Much has been written of how marginalized regions recreate and are created by their stereotypical pasts. Like their counterparts in Appalachia, the highlands of Scotland, and other places on the edge of modern centers, residents of Cape Breton Island have a strong sense of who they are and what makes them different but valuable. They use their "folk" identity to remind themselves and the mainlanders that they are special, but at the same time they put themselves (or in some cases their neighbors) down as backwards and dependent. There is no room in the "traditional" stories of Celtic clannishness or labor's solidarity for the influence of modern industrial forms and structures.

People who live on the margins are measured by their ability to keep up with the striving value systems of the "middle." Matthew Arnold, an icon of early educational criticism, once said that it was the middle class of the modern age who were "barbarians" because they held political and economic control and were obsessed with the mere accumulation of material goods. At the height of the Industrial Revolution, he called for "an expansion of consciousness that would give people a fuller grasp of the ideal intellectual and aesthetic potential of the human spirit" (Stein, 1986, 25). If becoming more like the middle means becoming another kind of barbarian, then perhaps Cape Bretoners and other margin dwellers are better off with their own sense of idealistic self-worth. Although there is poverty, health issues, and a lack of resources for families and children, Cape Bretoners are not victims, ignorant peasants passed by modernity, or rebellious highlanders. Cape Bretoners are not passive recipients of external knowledge, nor are they lacking in modern sensibilities, but their relationship with tradition is complex.

For example, one of the selling points of Cape Breton is its Gaelic culture—language, music, and dance. Highland dancing has experienced a resurgence across North America, and towns like Glace Bay have not been excluded. The immigrant families of the colliery towns, however, may not have had Scottish roots, but as the popularity of things Celtic increased nationally, local families joined in. I tried to take advantage of this myself, while in Glace Bay, by taking Gaelic and fiddling classes at UCCB. One of my older friends was dismayed. "Why do you want to learn such a dirty language?" she asked me. As a young girl, she had experienced the pain of her classmates who still spoke Gaelic when they were in school and were chastised by the teachers to speak English. When she was little, Gaelic had been "dirty" much the same way that speaking Ukrainian or Italian would have been discouraged. She politely said little of my efforts to play the fiddle but was quick to tell me about concerts in the area to which her friends who were interested in traditional music were going.

I attended such a concert in Glace Bay featuring Natalie MacMaster, a Cape Breton musician famous for her precocious talent. The concert was excellent. It was her first solo concert as the lead musician, and the crowd was a big one. The social demographics of the people in the audience varied tremendously from country folk to townspeople. As I looked around the concert hall, I recognized a variety of local residents from what I would call more affluent families (most of them worked in Sydney or in government jobs). The couple with whom I came was among this group, two seniors who had both had successful careers as educators in the town. The concert was held at the recently renovated Savoy Theatre, and my companions were sponsors, a group called "Friends of the Arts." There were also a number of clergy in the crowd and some people I recognized from the staff at UCCB.

As the mayor had said in an earlier interview (he was also there), "The people here really know how to have fun!" The toe tapping and clapping showed how vigorously the crowd enjoyed the traditional music. Country music was popular in the town, if the radio stations were any indication, but local talent like Natalie MacMaster gave a local flavor to the usual Nashville performers. The support of folk music allows more affluent residents to be "cultural" while also maintaining the local "folk" identity. Pensioners returning to Cape Breton after retirement could also appreciate the traditional "folk" culture because of the development of their Cape Breton identity while living away. Besides, everyone appreciates a good tune. With the growth of heritage industries across Canada (and the United States), the local identity of Glace Bay as a place of country comforts, embodied in young Natalie MacMaster's artful fiddling, was supported by a diverse set of residents.

The myth of community, however, was difficult to maintain—even in moments of making music. Although residents of the Bay had a great deal in common, as unemployment became more and more acute, class divisions between those who had jobs and those that did not became more difficult to hide. The "folk" image of the town had increased with the emphasis on promoting Cape Breton "heritage" and the colliery town history. How much, however, did the auditorium full of toe-tapping pensioners, clergy, university staff, the mayor, and an anthropologist from the States represent the "folk" of Glace Bay? As the disparities in income continued to increase, low-income residents of the town had less and less in common with the coal miners' "heritage" being sold down the street at the Miners' Museum and the talented young fiddlers from Mabou playing tunes for middle-class members of the new municipality.

Living "Away"
In the past, especially during the 1950s and through the 1970s, individuals left Glace Bay and made homes off-island in two very distinct paths, either as professionals with formal postsecondary degrees or as laborers, often with only high school diplomas or less. Glace Bay residents either used their educational credentials to acquire jobs within the town or left to pursue professional careers in Halifax, Boston, Montreal, Toronto, Calgary, and even Los Angeles. With the decline of the coal and steel industries in the late sixties, people also left the region en masse to pursue available working-class jobs in central Canada. The extended community of Glace Bay living outside the region, therefore, had distinct class differences. In looking back at the town, however, emigrants from Glace Bay imagined their home in much the same way as local residents did. They reconstructed shared images that served to provide comfort and a sense of identity, regardless of whether their perspective came from a blue-collar job in Kitchener, Ontario, or a law office in Halifax.

I learned how two factory workers, Cape Bretoners living "away" in Kitchener, Ontario, played a part in constructing the folk image of their home by maintaining their Glace Bay "literacy." The two men were brothers who moved to Ontario from Cape Breton as teenagers. They both married women from the Maritimes, belonged to social groups made up predominantly of Maritimers, and in the summer went on vacation with a group of emigrant Glace Bay "Boys." They were social members of the Canadian Legion but did not vote, union members but not leaders, and had extended families of their own in Ontario but visited their mother in Glace Bay every summer they could afford to do so. Although they claimed to know little of Glace Bay since they had been away so long, when they introduced me to their friends, the importance of their Glace Bay identity became clear.

I was introduced as the girl who was staying with their mother back home. They then reminded their friends (in this case the crowd having a beer after work at the Legion) that they were from Glace Bay. They asked me what I had come to know as the typical questions: Had I had the lobster? Had I been down in the pit? Had I been to a bingo game?

Didn't I find the Glace Bay people friendly? These questions and the explanations they gave along with them demonstrated to me that although these two men had not lived in Glace Bay for thirty years, they still maintained their proficiency in "local knowledge." In a sense, they still knew and could tell the appropriate "folk tales."

Cape Bretoners who left the island and found economic success in middle-class social groups had a different view of Glace Bay. One woman I spoke with lived in a high-rise apartment building just outside of Toronto and was married to a successful contractor. She visited her mother in Glace Bay every other year or so and told me that she looked forward to going "home" every chance she gets. Cape Breton is beautiful, she explained, and she enjoyed the family closeness there. When I asked if she associated with Cape Bretoners in Ontario, she said no. Her identity as a middle-class matron was reflected in her bridge group and club memberships. She listened to Cape Breton music, she said, but not because she remembered it from growing up. When she visited, she joked, it was as a tourist, buying souvenirs and watching the natives dance. Outside of her mother's house, she told me, she felt slightly uncomfortable. She did not know how to get along anymore, she said, and she had very few friends still living in the Bay.

I asked this Toronto resident about her education in Glace Bay. She told me that education was of supreme value; going to school and graduating was her mother's greatest wish for her. But, she said, education was for going away, to give you the tools to survive elsewhere. To get along at home, she explained, you needed to know how to do things the Glace Bay way, and it was that knowledge she felt she had lost, even though she visited often. The two brothers in Kitchener, on the other hand, said they felt very comfortable at home in Cape Breton. They did not know as many people, they explained, but the family would get together, or they'd go down to the hall and have a beer and it would be great to be home.

The phenomenon of a "folk" identity, applied from both within and without, is a double-edged sword. Constructing a "simpler life" to help make adversity easier to stand can cause Cape Bretoners, despite their modern lifestyles and industrial production, to be treated like and to identify themselves as an idealized "folk." This image, while useful for maintaining cohesiveness in a community that watches at least a third of each high school class emigrate, is antithetical to progress in a global economy.

As folk wisdom, common sense is important in towns like Glace Bay because it fits into two images that are consistent with the local identity. Common sense is both experiential, reflecting the working-class, subsistence nature of a coal town, and colloquial, calling upon images of a "folk" living in a closely knit community. School knowledge and concepts of economic development, conversely, are distant, formal, and based upon abstractions beyond the experiences of local residents. Despite their strong value of schooling, what was key was not how education was valued but how that value was expressed when knowledge was called into question in everyday settings.

Imported Knowledge
Regional leaders, however, did not consider common sense the key to revitalizing Cape Breton's economy. Jackie Scott, the president of UCCB, advocated bringing in an "elite" to the region, what she defined as highly educated, entrepreneurial individuals who will bring with them postindustrial employment opportunities that can sustain the island economy. I asked if this solution would only exacerbate the problem of the region not supporting its own, welcoming returning children but not supporting those who stay at home. She replied that there are two problems with "those that stay" (a comment that I found ironic since her institution serves this population). On a meritocratic level, she explained, individuals who never leave the region do not receive the life experience needed to compete in the larger economy. "They do not have the comparative perspective," she said, "of what is 'normal'." My research questions this point in the extent of knowledge sought out by local residents through self-educating practices of reading and engaging in global media sources, but many of these self-educated Cape Bretoners would agree with her. Dr. Scott's second point was that those individuals who stay at home often fall into the mentality of "tribal behavior" that she felt was characteristic of the region, which she defined as "driving toward the mean, distrusting those that rise above." She attributed this characteristic to the area's union legacy as part of the industrial model that chokes the island's economy. There was also, she continued, a distrust of those who are no longer dependent on the community's fate as their own. "In other words, they are no longer dependent on that which the community depends...the government or the company."

Cape Bretoners, like the peoples of Appalachia and other marginalized regions of North America, are accused by politicians, economic developers and even themselves as being closed minded about the possibilities of economic progress. This "backward" portrayal is reinforced and in some ways produced by sterotypical views of the region, a portrayal to which local residents are not immune (Billings, Norman, and Ledford, 1999). One of the town leaders echoed Dr. Scott's analysis:

> People are naive. They're ignorant of the real world, of how things really are in the economy. Part of this is due to the media...what they see is not what they can get...nor is it likely for most.

There are, nevertheless, daily examples of personal success as defined by local values of clannishness, fun, and collegiality. Those same values of clannishness and collegiality, however, do lead to the "tribal behavior" of tearing down those who get ahead. The residents of Glace Bay have much in common with marginalized regions around the world in that they have little control over economic and political decisions that affect their futures. In this case, education has not improved empowerment. This failure to gain economic security or political power through education has led to a cynical and sometimes defeatist attitude toward academic challenge.

Local Learning
Early emphasis in Glace Bay on the development of not only schools for children but also on study groups, labor education, reading, and the widespread practice of discussion and debate demonstrate that individuals within the town believed that the pursuit of knowledge was not only a necessary component of economic success but also a fundamental practice of living in a progressive society. While in no way resistant to a middle-class success ideology, the pursuit of learning for the sake of learning allowed for resistance to the conditions of capitalism that made life difficult for the industrial worker.

In resisting the company through striking or, in more recent times, in complaining about and contesting the efficacy of training for jobs that don't exist, the residents of Glace Bay interpreted their educational opportunities and constraints through their own frameworks of meaning. As Yngvesson said, "subversion is not subjection" (1993). The people of Glace Bay were not ignorant of educational opportunity, nor were they blind to the needs of seeking new knowledge and skills for survival. When John MacEachern spoke of the need to develop a culture of learning, he needed only to listen and watch as his neighbors and friends actively pursued learning opportunities on a local basis. What was needed, perhaps, was to develop existing values of local learning to external contexts and, through that application, gain more autonomy and authority over the future.

To learn, to grow, to become better than before can be useful not only to the individual but transformative to the conditions of those around her or him. The man who stood holding a baby to argue in defense of his education put into words what many others had implied, that their own success would help others in their family and community. Striving for gains, as Carnoy (1987) puts it, is not an individualized endeavor but is always connected to the lived experiences of the individual, which are inherently social. In striving for a university degree or a medical technician's certificate, individuals do not act alone. Their education is always framed within the context of cultural values and relationships. If they find it necessary to leave the town to find work, they leave families and friends behind them. Education, in this case, is a process of transformation that must have fellowship. Again, the dialogic nature of learning in the town and the emphasis on the uses of knowledge in public and private settings reiterate the importance of the cultural processes of learning. Local knowledge in Glace Bay was affirmed as useful because it could be shared, bartered in some cases, but otherwise made part of the local wisdom of the community. How can local wisdom be used in productive ways as it is when focused on local problems to address regional challenges? The "tribal" aspect of relationships within the town was used effectively to nurture and support in times of trouble, but how might such values be applied to sustainable community development for the future?

Father Greg MacLeod, director of the Tompkin's Institute and New Dawn Community Development Corporation (both part of the cooperative movement in Cape Breton and legacies of the Antigonish Movement), argued in a series of white papers and films produced in the 1980s and 1990s that development strategies for the unemployed have to be cooperative projects rather than training initiatives for individuals. "I am responsible for my neighbor who is unemployed," he states in one of his documentaries about the cooperative movement. Education is about opening up learning opportunities and changing the individual, he states, and building a full and abundant life for everyone. Like the labor leaders of the early part of the century, MacLeod refers to education as a tool for empowerment as well as employment. Such empowerment, he insists, will aid these communities in crisis more so than training for jobs that do not exist.

MacLeod's call for community development and community-based education did not have much effect on policymakers who had benefited from the resources gained by importing outside expertise and credentials. As a result of shifts from industrial development to entrepreneurial development and retraining, education had become big business in Cape Breton. UCCB and other postsecondary institutions in the area contributed to the job market as well as providing training. The development of education as a commodity and the accompanying employment that the education market generates were accepted positively despite the emphasis on revenue as well as learning. The positive value of the efficacy of education for success, although challenged by the reduced return on investment in the fragile economy, allowed for the unquestioned expansion of educational businesses like training centers and consulting firms over the past three decades. Because they were built on positive assumptions held toward schooling and learning, these businesses benefited from the locally held value of education as a positive cultural practice.

Grassroots community development in Glace Bay has been tried. In an interview with another development officer regarding an initiative to garner public opinion regarding development strategies, numerous attempts to set up mass meetings failed because of a lack of attendance and active participation by those who did show up in constructing specific goals or objectives. At the mass meetings, the director told me, "They did nothing but complain and eat the free sandwiches!" In a public forum, almost all public officials told me in discouragement about the complaining and negativity of local residents toward their future. Despite his frustration at trying to initiate grassroots support, the development officer quoted above was positive about his resolve. "I won't leave," he said, "we've got to find a way to make this work for us, for our children!"

In my interview conversations, however, most people did not complain so much as try to express their discomfort with not having any answers. One of the recently displaced fishermen explained how difficult he felt it was to answer such requests for information:

> You see we don't know what we want. It's not that we're foolish, it's just that things have always kind of been the way they are. We're survivors. It's hard to look ahead when you're just trying to hang on. Some people have got

it OK, good for them...but it's hard to tell you what kind of education we need or what kind of grant project would do the trick.

Passivity does not accurately describe reactions like this. Perhaps a sad frustration is more appropriate.

Death of the King
Six years after leaving Cape Breton, I returned to Glace Bay with my baby daughter and husband to visit friends and see what had changed in the region. Two weeks before we arrived, the government announced the closing of the last coal mine in Cape Breton. This was the death knoll that many people had talked about during my fieldwork. Coal will never die completely, some had said. Others believed it was only a matter of time. The latter group was right. Aside from the pit closings, a lot had changed, but unemployment was still high and jobs hard to find. The environmental wear and tear of hundred years of coal mining and steel production had come to the fore as local residents began to get reports of ground and water contamination from the Sydney Tar Ponds.[1] There were some improvements. The community college system had received a shot of energy from new management, and there seemed to be more proactive training and unemployment services, but the more I talked to people the more I realized the question I had come to ask about Glace Bay and towns like it had not changed. Education as a panacea for community development and individual advancement was still prevalent in public rhetoric, but the question "Training for what?" was still unanswered.

The study of post-compulsory education has much to learn from communities like Glace Bay. As more and more individuals turn to education as a strategy for negotiating a knowledge economy, institutions of postsecondary education and government policymakers who provide support for educational initiatives must be aware of both the reproductive and productive possibilities of those strategies. Learning is no burden to carry if the outcome of that learning can be made positive and productive. If not, the legitimacy of that learning is questioned. "Training for what?" is not just being asked in Glace Bay. In any area in which the economic opportunities do not match educational achievements, the efficacy of schooling is questioned.

The multiple literacies with which individuals negotiated diverse social contexts both within the town and outside of it may be key to the development of viable economic alternatives in the future. Local wisdom includes complex networks of shared information as well as personal explorations of self-improvement. Residents of Glace Bay unanimously advocated the need for education for economic development. At the same time they saw the negative aspects of that strategy and questioned formal education's effectiveness. Perhaps there are ways to use informal practices of knowledge acquisition and transmission to empower locally based economic development. Perhaps in programs such as community studies at UCCB or the professional development of fishing cooperatives, there are ways to break down the boundaries of formal systems of post-compulsory education to take advantage of regional practices of inquiry and knowledge production.

Self-sufficiency is required for sustainable development in Glace Bay. Self-sufficiency arises from the ability to engage in dialogue both externally and internally for all members of the community. In applying the notion of education as a development strategy, policymakers in the Maritime region build upon both a success ethic of modernity and the underlying ideology of self-improvement constructed on principles of labor activism and cultural values of local literacy. To be successful, however, in Glace Bay is not to train for jobs that don't exist but to improve oneself in ways that fulfill the human spirit as well as economic necessity. It is not enough, I believe, for Glace Bay people to live in quiet desperation, scratching for the few jobs available, without also creating opportunities for personal and social success. Education as a development strategy needs to be actualized in ways that reach beyond development grants for post-compulsory training to create a definition of education which highlights the individual's potential for growth within the community as well as the nation.

Note

1 The Tar Ponds refers to the area surrounding the steel mill on the southwest side of Sydney affected by the steel industry. Other issues include the lack of appropriate sewage disposal throughout the area and an aging public infrastructure.

BIBLIOGRAPHY

Anderson, B. (1983). *Imagined communities*. New York: Verso.

Apple, M. W. (Ed.) (1982). *Cultural and economic reproduction in education: Essays on class, ideology, and the state*. Boston: Routledge.

Apple, M. W., and L. Weis (eds.) (1983). *Ideology and practice in schooling*. Philadelphia: Temple University Press.

Axelrod, P. (1990). *Making a middle class: Student life in English Canada during the thirties*. Montreal: McGill-Queen's University Press.

Axelrod, P. (1989). Introduction. In Axelrod, P., and John G. Reid, (eds.), *Youth, university, and Canadian society: Essays in the social history of higher education*. Kingston, ON: McGill-Queen's University Press.

Barlow, M., and H.J. Robertson (1994). *Class warfare: The assault on Canada's schools*. Toronto: Key Porter Books.

Bedard, K. (2001). Human capital versus signaling models: University access and high school dropouts, *Journal of Political Economy*, 109(4) 749–76.

Bernstein, B. B. (1975). *Class and pedagogies: Visible and invisible.* Paris: OECD.

Billings, D., G. Norman, and K. Ledford (1999). *Confronting Appalachian stereotypes: Back talk from an American region.* Lexington: University Press of Kentucky.

Bledstein, B. J. (1976). *The culture of professionalism: The middle class and the development of higher education in America.* New York: Norton.

Bodnar, J. (1989). Power and memory in oral history: Workers and managers at Studebaker, *The Journal of American History,* 75(4) 1201–1221.

Bourdieu, P. (1990). *The logic of practice.* Stanford, CA: Stanford University Press.

_____ (1977). Cultural reproduction and social reproduction. In Karabel, Jerome, and A. H. Halsey (eds.), *Power and ideology in education.* New York: Oxford University Press.

Bourdieu, P. and L. J. D. Wacquant (1992). *Introduction to reflexive sociology.* Cambridge: Polity Press.

Brint, S. and J. Karabel (1989). *The diverted dream: Community colleges and the promise of educational opportunity in America, 1900–1985.* New York: Oxford University Press.

Brown, K. (1994). *Strategic economic action plan, August 12, 1994.* Sydney, NS: Cape Breton County Economic Development Authority.

Campbell, D. F. (1973). Address to Sydney Rotary Club, November 6. University College of Cape Breton Bras d'Or Collection.

Carnoy, M. (1993). *The new global economy in the information age: Reflections on our changing world.* University Park, PA: Pennsylvania State University Press.

Carnoy, M. (1987). *Higher education and graduate employment in India: A summary of three case studies.* Paris: International Institute for Educational Planning.

Collins, R. (1979). *The credential society.* New York: Academic Press.

Dougherty, K. J. (1994). *The contradictory college: The conflicting origins, impacts, and futures of the community college.* Albany, NY: State University of New York Press.

Drucker, P. F. (1993). *Post-capitalist society.* New York: HarperCollins.

Dunn, C. W. (1991). *Highland settler: A portrait of the Scottish Gael in Cape Breton and Eastern Nova Scotia.* Wreck Cove, NS: Breton Books.

Eller, R. (1982). *Miners, millhands, and mountaineers: Industrialization of the Appalachian South, 1880–1930.* Knoxville: University of Tennessee Press.

Freire, P. (1994). *Pedagogy of hope: Reliving pedagogy of the oppressed.* Translated by Robert R. Barr. New York: Continuum.

Freire, P. (1985). *The politics of education: Culture, power, and liberation.* Translated by Donaldo Macedo. South Hadley, MA: Bergin & Garvey.

Freire, P. (1970). *Pedagogy of the oppressed.* New York: Continuum Publishing.

Friesen, G. (1994). Adult education and union education: Aspects of English Canadian cultural history in the 20th century, *Labour/LeTravail*, 34(Fall), 163–88.

Gabbard, D. (1998). Decolonizing society, *Peace Review*, 10(1), 107.

Geertz, C. (1983). *Local knowledge: Further essays in interpretive anthropology.* Basic Books.

Giddens, A. (1994). Living in a post-traditional society. In, Beck, U., A. Giddens, and S. Lash (eds.), *Reflexive modernization: Politics, tradition and aesthetics in the modern social order.* Stanford, CA: Stanford University Press.

Gold, J. R. and M. Gold (1995). *Imagining Scotland: Tradition, representation and promotion in Scottish tourism since 1750.* Hants, England: Ashgate Publishing Co.

Gouldner, A. W. (1979). *The future of intellectuals and the rise of the new class.* New York: Macmillan & Co.

Grant, J. N. (1980). *Black Nova Scotians.* Halifax, NS: Nova Scotia Museum as part of the Department of Education, Province of Nova Scotia.

Greenhouse, C. J., B. Yngvesson, and D. M. Engel (1994). *Law and community in three American towns.* Ithaca: Cornell University Press.

Handelman, D. (1982). "Inside-out, outside-in: Concealment and revelation in Newfoundland Christmas mumming." In Bruner, E. (ed.), *Text, play, and story: The construction and reconstruction of self and society.* Boulder, CO: Waveland Press.

Harrison, J. F. C. (1961). *Learning and living: 1790–1960: A study of the history of the English adult education movement.* London: Rivers Oram Press.

Harvey, D. (2000). *Spaces of hope.* Berkeley, CA: University of California Press.

Lipset, S. M. (1989). *Continental divide: The values and institutions of the United States and Canada.* New York: Routledge.

MacDonald, C. S. (1951). *50 Years: Town of Glace Bay fiftieth anniversary.* Glace Bay, NS.

MacEwan, P. (1976). *Miners and steelworkers: Labour in Cape Breton.* Toronto: Samuel Stevens Hakkert and Co.

MacLeod, J. (1995). *Ain't no makin' it: Aspirations and attainment in a low-income neighborhood.* Boulder, CO: Westview Press.

Marshall, J. (1990). Literacy and people's power in a mozambican factory, *Comparative Education Review*, 34(1), 61–84.

McGilly, F. (1993). *An introduction to Canada's public social services: Understanding income and health programs.* Toronto: McClelland & Steward, Inc.

McKay, I. (1994). *The quest of the folk.* Montreal: McGill-Queen's University Press.

Mellor, J. (1983). *The company store: J. B. McLachlan and the Cape Breton coal miners 1900–1925.* Toronto: Doubleday.

Merry, S. (1991). *Getting justice and getting even: Legal consciousness among working-class Americans.* Chicago: University of Chicago Press.

Mills, C. W. (1956). *The sociological imagination.* New York: Oxford University Press.

Morris, M. (1936). *William Morris: Artist, writer, socialist.* Volume 2: Morris as a socialist. Oxford: Basil Blackwell.

Nash, J. (1989). *From tanktown to high tech: The clash of community and industrial cycles.* New York: State University of New York Press.

Newton, D. (1992). *Where coal is king: The story of the Cape Breton Miners' Museum.* Glace Bay, NS: Cape Breton Miners' Foundation.

Ong, W. J. (1982). *Orality and literacy: The technologizing of the word.* New York: Routledge.

Ortner, S. (1991). Identities: The hidden life of class, *Journal of Anthropological Research,* 54(1), 1.

Pappas, G. (1989). *Magic city: Unemployment in a working-class community.* Ithaca, NY: Cornell University Press.

Pomponio, A., and D. Lancy (1986). A pen or a bushknife? School, work, and "personal investment" in Papua New Guinea, *Anthropology and Education Quarterly,* 17(1), 40–61.

Radway, J. (1984). *Reading the romance: Women, patriarchy and popular literature.* Chapel Hill, NC: University of North Carolina Press.

Raissiguier, C. (1994). *Becoming women, becoming workers: Identity formation in a French vocational school.* Albany: State University of New York Press.

Riemer, F. (1997). From welfare to working poor: Prioritizing practice in research on employment-training programs for the poor, *Anthropology and Education Quarterly,* 28(1), 85–110.

Robbins, D. (1998). "The need for an epistemological "Break", in Grenfell, M., and D. James (eds.), *Bourdieu and education: Acts of practical theory.* London: Falmer Press.

Sassen, S. (1991). *The global city: New York, London, Tokyo.* Princeton, NJ: Princeton University Press.

Stein, R. (1986). *In pursuit of beauty: The aesthetic movement in America.* Chicago: University of Chicago Press.

University College of Cape Breton (1970, September). *Report to the Governors.* University College of Cape Breton Bras d'Or Collection.

Veysey, L. R. (1965). *The emergence of the American university.* Chicago: University of Chicago Press.

Wallace, A. F. C. (1981). *St. Clair: A nineteenth-century coal town's experience with a disaster-prone industry.* Ithaca, NY: Cornell University Press.

Watson, L., and M. B. Watson-Franke (1985). *Interpreting life histories: An anthropological inquiry.* New Brunswick, NJ: Rutgers University Press.

Weis, L. (1990). *Working class without work: High school students in a de-industrializing economy.* New York: Routledge.

Wexler, P. (1987). *Social analysis of education: After the new sociology.* New York: Routledge.

Williams, R. (1973). *The country and the city.* Oxford: Oxford University Press.

Willis, P. (1977). *Learning to labor.* Aldershot: Gower.

Yngvesson, B. (1993). *Virtuous citizens, disruptive subjects: Order and complaint in a New England court.* New York: Routledge.

Statistics Canada (1991). Cat. No. 95-312

(10 October, 1931). *The Sydney Post Record*

(26 October 1938). *The Sydney Post Record*

Index

Acadia, 54-55
Adult Vocational Training Center (AVTC), 82
Anderson, B., 21-22
Antigonish Movement, 52, 73,
Arnold, Matthew, 12979, 135
Atlantic Groundfish Strategy, The (TAGS), 80, 84-91, 121
Bachelor of Arts in Community Studies (BACS), 65-66
Barlow, Maude, 7
Bingo, 100-101
Bodnar, J., 126
Bourdieu, P., 3, 9, 44
British Empire Steel and Coal Corporation (BESCO), 53
Cape Breton, 6-8, 12, 16, 17-18, 27, 30-31, 36, 39-40, 72-73, 80, 85-86, 91, 94, 97-98, 127-129
   Economic development, 6-8, 17-18, 27, 72-73, 80, 85-86, 91, 94, 97
   Identity, 12, 36, 39-40, 98, 127-129
   Immigrants, 30-31
   Municipality of, 16
Cape Breton Community College (CBCC), 82
Cape Breton Development Corporation (DEVCO), 26-28, 72
Cape Breton Post, The, 48
Capitalism, 3, 6-7, 12, 23
Carnoy, M., 135
Ceilidhs, 30, 128
Coastal Courier, The, 48
Cohen, Fanny, 47
Community college, 41, 82
Compucollege, 59, 82
Consciousness, 9-10
   Educational, 9-10
   Legal, 9-10
Conservative Party, 26
Cultural capital, 44, 46, 101
Dalhousie, 52, 55
Delany, Ida, 52
De-industrialization, 8, 39, 91
Donkin, 29

Dominion Coal and Steel
    Corporation (DOSCO), 26,
    34, 53, 56
Education, 4-5, 7, 10-11, 14, 41,
    51-52, 54, 57-58, 61, 64-65,
    68, 81, 138
    achievement levels, 54, 68
    and adult education, 51-52,
    81
    as community contribution,
    65
    as democratic, 7, 41
    as power, 4, 10
    as regional development
    tool, 4, 14, 138
    aspirations, 11, 52, 57-58,
    61, 64
    brain drain (out-migration),
    5
Entrepreneurship training, 78
Freire, P., 9, 66
Gabarus, 49
Gaelic, 1, 12-13, 31, 129
    Culture, 12, 13, 31, 129
    Language, 1, 31
Geertz, Clifford, 98, 109
Giddens, A., 125
Higher education in Canada, 53,
    72
Illich, I. 14, 100
Labor unions, 24-27, 39, 111,
    113, 121
Lancy, D., 67
Lingan, 26
MacEachern, John, 120, 135
MacKenzie College, 59, 82
MacLeod, 11, 32, 44, 58
MacNeil, Rita, 13
Magi Learning Centre, 78

McLachlan, J.B., 46
Mellor, J., 46
Merry, S., 9,10
Miller, Tom, 120-121
Miner's Museum, 33, 120, 126,
    131
Morris, William, 6-7
Morrison Glace Bay High
    School, 54, 59, 62
Mount Alison, 54-55
Nash, J., 27-28
Nash, Herbie, 111
New Aberdeen, 26, 34
New Democratic Party (NDP),
    26
New Waterford, 26
Newfoundland, 12-13, 19
Nova Scotia, 19, 23, 30, 33, 76
Nova Scotia Eastern Institute of
    Technology, 64
Paschendaele, 47
Pogie (see unemployment
    insurance), 14, 58, 61, 75,
    77, 79, 93
Pomponio, A., 67
Post-secondary education, 8, 14,
    50, 54, 60, 63, 65-66, 71,
    73, 77, 80-81, 133
    and institutions in Cape
Breton, 60
    and technology programs,
    66, 73
    traditional
    knowledge/wisdom, 14, 133
    training programs, 8, 50, 54,
    63, 65, 71, 77
    tuition, 80-81
Public library, 47

Reading (importance of), 46, 49, 98
Religion, 32
Resistance theory, 43, 45
Riemer, F., 91
Robertson, Heather Jane, 7
Royal Canadian Mounted Police (RCMP), 76
St. Francis Xavier University, 51-54, 64
St. Michael's High School, 57
Sassen, Saskia, 2
Social reproduction, 43, 45
Social stratification, 11, 41
Superstition of rarity, 6-7
Sydney Post-Record, The, 50
Tourism, 12, 23, 28-30, 98
Unemployment insurance, 14, 58, 61, 75, 77, 79, 93
Unemployment rate, 58, 73, 79
University-College of Cape Breton (UCCB), 54, 64, 77, 107-108, 110, 118, 130, 136, 138
University of Toronto, 52
Wallace, A.F.C., 47
Willis, Paul, 43-44
Women, 33-36, 48
Yngvesson, B., 10, 40, 134

General Editor: Norm Denzin

Cultural Critique is a research monograph series drawing from those scholarly traditions in the social sciences and the humanities that are premised on critical, performance-based cultural studies agenda. Preference is given to experimental, risk-taking manuscripts that are at the intersection of interpretative theory, critical methodology, culture, media, history, biography, and social structure. Asserting that culture is best understood as a gendered performance, this international-research monograph series combines ethnography and critical textual approaches to the study of popular literature, media, myth, advertising, religion, science, cinema, television, and the new communication and information technologies. This new series creates a space for the study of those global cultural practices and forms that shape the meanings of self, identity, race, ethnicity, class, nationality, and gender in the contemporary world.

Preference will be given to authors who engage a variety of critical qualitative, interpretive methodologies, from semiotics and critical textual analysis to interpretive and auto-ethnography, personal narrative, and the practices of investigative, civic, intimate, and immersion journalism. We seek non-conventional, experimental manuscripts. Qualitative methods are material and interpretive practices. They do not stand outside politics and cultural criticism. Critical methodologies advance the project of moral criticism. This spirit, critically imagining and pursuing a more democratic society, has been a guiding feature of cultural studies from the very beginning. Contributors to *Cultural Critique* will forward this project. They will take up such methodological and moral issues as the local and global, text and context, voice, writing for the other, and the author presence in the text. *Cultural Critique* understands that the discourses of a critical, moral methodology are basic to any effort to re-engage the promise of the social sciences for democracy in the twenty-first century. *Cultural Critique* will publish works of ethnopoetry, auto-ethnography, creative non-fiction, performance texts, book reviews, and critical analyses of current media representations and formations. Projected contents (and contributors) will be drawn from scholarly traditions in the social sciences and humanities, including history, anthropology, sociology, communications, art history, education, American studies, kinesiology, performance studies, and English. The scope of submissions will be international.

For additional information about this series or for the submission of manuscripts, please contact:

> Dr. Norm Denzin
> University of Illinois, Institute of Communications Research
> 228 Gregory Hall, 810 So. Wright Street
> Urbana, IL 61801

To order other books in this series, please contact our Customer Service Department:

> (800) 770-LANG (within the U.S.)
> (212) 647-7706 (outside the U.S.)
> (212) 647-7707 FAX

or browse online by series:

WWW.PETERLANGUSA.COM